Praise for *Shakespeare on Toast*

' Crystal's witty and engaging book is a relaxed, user-
 dly reminder that enjoying Shakespeare should be as
 as breathing.' Dominic Dromgoole, Artistic Director
o. Shakespeare's Globe

'A brilliantly enjoyable, light hearted look at Shakespeare
which dispels the myths and makes him accessible to all. I
love it!' Judi Dench

'Ben Crystal's excellent book is an ideal way to gain an
understanding of why Shakespeare is so brilliant and so
 yable.' Sir Richard Eyre

 asterclass for modern beginners and old hands alike.'
 Times

'H morous, unpretentious and fascinating.' *Independent*
 Sunday

' asty snack with genius ... Having Crystal as a compan-
 through the stickier parts of *Hamlet* and *Macbeth* is like
 oing to the theatre with an intelligent friend ... Crystal
 ries his damnedest as an actor, scholar and Shakespeare's
 biggest fan to demystify the Bard for doubting 21st-century
 theatre-phobics.' Katy Guest, *Independent*

SHAKESPEARE ON TOAST

GETTING A TASTE FOR THE BARD

BEN CRYSTAL

ICON BOOKS

Distributed in the UK, Europe, South Africa and Asia
by TBS Ltd, TBS Distribution Centre, Colchester Road,
Frating Green, Colchester CO7 7DW

This edition published in Australia in 2009 by Allen & Unwin Pty Ltd,
PO Box 8500, 83 Alexander Street, Crows Nest, NSW 2065

Distributed in Canada by Penguin Books Canada,
90 Eglinton Avenue East, Suite 700, Toronto, Ontario M4P 2YE

ISBN: 978-184831-054-4

Typesetting in 11pt Minion by Wayzgoose

Printed and bound in the UK by
CPI Mackays, Chatham ME5 8TD

Contents

About the author

Ben Crystal is an actor and writer. He studied English Language and Linguistics at Lancaster University before training at Drama Studio London. He has worked in TV, film and theatre, including the reconstructed Shakespeare's Globe, London, and is a narrator for RNIB Talking Books, Channel 4 and the BBC. He co-wrote *Shakespeare's Words* (Penguin 2002) and *The Shakespeare Miscellany* (Penguin 2005) with David Crystal, and regularly gives talks and workshops on Shakespeare.

He lives in London, and online at www.bencrystal.com

Prologue

Never, never, never, never, never.

King Lear, Act 5, Scene 3, line 306

That quote is one of the most stunning lines in Shakespeare, and after reading this book you'll be able to give a number of very good reasons why this is true.

But first and foremost: this book is not a number of things.

This book is not a particularly 'actorly' book, full of stories of acting Shakespeare. There are plenty of other books out there full of fabulous anecdotes about acting Shakespeare.

Nor is this really a scholarly book, full of incredibly complicated analyses of structures and themes that may (or may not) be in Shakespeare's plays. There are plenty of academic books already out there too.

When I began to write this book, I looked around to see if anyone else had already done a similar thing, and while there are plenty of quite tricky, advanced books on Shakespeare, and plenty of 'Shakespeare Made Easy'-type books, there didn't seem to be one that tried to make Shakespeare's plays accessible without dumbing them down.

There are also dozens of 'Introductions to Shakespeare'

available. I couldn't find a single one that shows the reader how to make Shakespeare their own; that once read, has given them the ability to go to any Shakespeare play and feel comfortable reading or watching it.

This book is certainly not the only way into Shakespeare.

But it is quick, easy, straightforward, and good for you. Just like beans on toast.

Act 1

Setting the Scene

Scene 1

Hollywood

Here's a thing: Shakespeare is partly responsible for the film career of Arnold Schwarzenegger.

Schwarzenegger got his first part in an American film (*Hercules in New York*) because Joe Weider, his friend and promoter, convinced the film's producers that Arnie had been a great Shakespearian actor in Austria, which, of course, he hadn't.

As it turns out, Weider's claim didn't end up being so far from the truth: in 1993, in the film *The Last Action Hero*, the world's biggest fan of the world's best action hero imagines Schwarzenegger as a *Terminator*-style Hamlet. The boy is watching Laurence Olivier in the 1948 *Hamlet*: Hamlet is about to kill Claudius – but hesitates, ponders the situation. 'Don't talk. Just do it!' the boy mutters at the screen. Suddenly, the muscle-bound Schwarzenegger has replaced Olivier:

HAMLET: Hey Claudius? You killed my father ... [*He picks Claudius up*] Big mistake! [*He throws Claudius through a stained-glass window; Claudius' body falls down a cliff*]

NARRATOR: Something is rotten in the state of Denmark, and Hamlet is taking out the trash! [*Multiple shots of Hamlet fighting and killing guards. He slices through a curtain with his sword to reveal Polonius standing behind it. Polonius pushes Hamlet's sword aside*]

POLONIUS: [*smiling*] Stay thy hand, fair prince.

HAMLET: Who said I'm fair? [*He shoots Polonius with an Uzi. Multiple shots of Hamlet walking through Elsinore castle, shooting soldiers with his Uzi*]

NARRATOR: No one is going to tell this sweet prince good night.

HAMLET: [*cigar in his mouth*] To be or not to be? [*taking out his lighter*] Not to be. [*lights his cigar, castle explodes*]

Schwarzenegger as Hamlet? Surprising, perhaps, but Shakespeare really does seem to get everywhere in this modern life. Slightly less surprising might be Shakespeare's part in the budding career of the young Sir John Gielgud, who became one of the most acclaimed Shakespearian actors of the 20th century.

Gielgud's first job as a professional actor was as a spear-carrier in a 1921 production of *Henry V*. One of the smallest parts in a play, a spear-carrier usually has very few lines (if any), and as the name suggests, the part requires the actor to stand still at the back of the stage, holding a spear/sword/

bowl of fruit, look pretty, and bow. Not to be discouraged by his measly one line, the young actor continued acting, and eight years later Gielgud performed what many people say was the greatest Hamlet ever.

Hamlet is considered to be the most sought-after and the most elusive role for actors, and the play remains the most produced of Shakespeare's works; countless productions, interpretations and re-interpretations have been dreamt up, trying to nail down The Definitive Hamlet. Schwarzenegger's, though, is the only one to have thrown Claudius out of a window.

Talk about character assassination.

Scene 2

A present-day street

Shakespeare invented the word *assassination*, a Bard-fact that will always boggle my mind. The word *assassin* has an 8th-century Arabic origin, but *assassination* is all Shakespeare.

Even-handed, far-off, hot-blooded, schooldays, well-respected are Shakespeare's too, as are *useful, moonbeam* and *subcontract.* If not for William S, we would be without *laughing yourself into stitches, setting your teeth on edge, not sleeping a wink, being cruel only to be kind,* and *playing fast and loose,* all adding to what turns out to be a very long list. In total, he introduced around 1,700 words and a horde of well-known phrases that we still use today.

Most of us would be happy if we added just one word to the language, never mind well over a thousand that last over 400 years.

Think (or Google) *assassination* and JFK comes up. Then, most likely, Abraham Lincoln, Martin Luther King and Julius Caesar. Their assassins are just as infamous: John Wilkes Booth, Lee Harvey Oswald, Brutus et al. Not to mention Guy Fawkes, one of the best-known (although failed) assassins, who attempted to blow up King James I and Parliament in November 1605.

Shortly after Fawkes' botched effort, Shakespeare wrote *Macbeth*, partly, some think, in response to the civil unrest of the time. *Macbeth* is also the play in which he coined the word *assassination*.

Now, in the early 21st century, Shakespeare really is everywhere.

Elvis quotes him in his No. 1 hit 'Are You Lonesome Tonight?' His plays are performed everywhere in countless languages. There have been productions using actors from all over the planet in the virtual computer world, *Second Life*. At the Edinburgh Fringe Festival in 2007 (which runs for only 22 days) there were over 30 productions, either of his plays or that used his plays as a starting point. And he's not just in theatres, of course.

Although the first film of a Shakespeare play (*King Lear*) was made way back in 1899, it's probably Baz Luhrmann's 1996 movie *Romeo + Juliet* that has done more in recent times than anything else to make Shakespeare more of a household name.

With 725 films to his name in March 2009, this writer from a small Warwickshire town four centuries ago is far and away the most prolific writer of movies: in 2005 alone, there were sixteen films made of his plays (never mind the thousands of fridge magnets, mugs and soft toys of his likeness).

The only writers with more screen credits to their names aren't writers of movies, but writers of soap operas. It's become a bit of a cliché to say it, but it's still true: if Shakespeare were alive today he'd be writing for the soaps rather than the movies or the theatre.

But more on that later.

A library

Despite this fame and apparent worldwide success, there's something about Shakespeare that makes him inaccessible to many people. It seems that

- § Shakespeare has become classed as high art – as litera-ture. He didn't start out that way. His plays were origin-ally the tools of actors; only much later were they books to read rather than plays to perform. Literature with a capital L has claimed him, and that acclaim has caused modern Shakespeare audiences either to revere or to hate him, neither of which are Good Things.

- § Shakespeare often appears cumbersome because it looks like he wrote in Olde English, which can make his plays seem to be full of unfamiliar words.

- § Shakespeare writes in poetry a fair amount of the time, and the very idea of 'poetry' puts a lot of people off. Not only that, but he uses a style of poetry that can be daunting just to look at.

The upshot of all this is that Shakespeare is often dumbed down and made 'accessible' by diluting, translating or rewriting his plays into modern English to try to draw people to his work. Either that or he's ignored in a cocktail of panic and preconception that he'll be too much hard work or just plain dull.

But Shakespeare is the man who made people believe there was an island owned by a magician (in *The Tempest*) and that statues could come to life by the power of love (in *The Winter's Tale*).

He's only Literature-with-a-capital-L until you put him back into context as an Elizabethan writer, not a 21st-century idol. Then, once you discover the key to it all, reading Shakespeare's poetry is a bit like following the clues in a Sherlock Holmes novel, or reading *The Da Vinci Code*: when you discover that he wrote his directions to his actors into the poetry, and work out how to decipher them, it all makes a lot more sense.

As for the words, well, admittedly, some of the words he uses might not have been in general use for a few hundred years, but a rather cooperative 95 per cent are words we know and use every day.

Hold that thought for a second: only 5 per cent of *all* the different words in *all* of Shakespeare's plays will give you a hard time. That means there's more contextual knowledge needed to watch an episode of the American political TV drama series *The West Wing* than there is to get through one of Shakespeare's plays.

The problem is, many give up by the time they get to the words. Successfully vault the Long Jump of Literature, stumble over the Pit of Poetry, take a quick look at the *actual words* he used, and the slightly odd spellings slam the final nail in the coffin. Whichever play has been briefly picked up is left once more to gather dust.

This isn't the way it has to be.

I'm going to show you how to read the instruction manual that is a Shakespeare play, because that's what they all are. Manuals, written by Shakespeare, for his actors, on how to perform great stories. It's the method that got me into the plays, and if it worked for me, who once wouldn't be seen dead near a production of Shakespeare, it'll work for you.

The key to it all is Theatre: both the space he wrote for and the event that the people were paying to see.

Stratford-upon-Avon

Context is *everything*, because no one knows who Shakespeare (the man) really was. Some of the very few absolute facts about the man himself that we know for definite are that

- There was once a man called William Shakespeare.

- He was born in Stratford-upon-Avon.

- He married Anne Hathaway, a girl at least seven years older than him, from his home town of Stratford-upon-Avon; they had three children together.

- He is buried in Stratford-upon-Avon.

- A number of really quite wonderful plays have been written under this name.

Add to that a few details of property we know he owned, of legal issues he was involved in, and half a dozen signatures. And that's all we've got. But no manuscripts – with the exception of a small part of a play, *Sir Thomas More*, thought to be written by Shakespeare – no notes, or diaries.

Nothing of consequence, in fact, that gives any indication as to what kind of man he was. Except his writing.

This isn't necessarily a bad thing, as far as we're concerned. It doesn't matter who Shakespeare might have been, because who he was isn't as important to us as *when* he was and *what* he did. But because so little about the man has been discovered, his life has become a bit of an enigma. And this seems to make people doubt that he wrote the plays.

This is not a rare thing. Almost nothing is known about the legendary blues guitarist and singer Robert Johnson (1911–38). Many consider him to be the king of the Delta blues singers, yet there are only two photos of him in existence, almost nothing is known about his early life, there are varying stories surrounding his death (the most popular being that his whisky was poisoned by a jealous juke joint owner, who'd caught Johnson flirting with his wife), and there are three different ideas about where he's buried. All we really have to go on are the 29 songs and a handful of alternative takes that he recorded. But he was so good, a legend has developed around him that he wasn't able to play the guitar until he went to a crossroads at midnight and the devil tuned his guitar for him. Not happy with the idea that he could naturally be that talented, people developed a magical reason for his talent. Just like Shakespeare.

Because the plays are held in such high regard, it's natural that we want to reveal the man behind them. So a lot of people have spent a lot of time trying to divine the man from his work, to find out who he was and what made him tick, in order to shed more light on the plays.

A number of authorities on Shakespeare alive today think Shakespeare's plays were written by 'someone else'. There's a comfort to be had from the idea that the mind behind greatness is regal, or rich – or better, a group of people. The contenders for authorship include Queen Elizabeth I, the playwright Christopher Marlowe, the Earl of Oxford, and Sir Francis Bacon. A couple of these contenders were, categorically, *dead while Shakespeare was still writing*, but I'm really not going to get into all that.

But I'd say there's a greater deal of comfort to be had from the idea that normal people can be geniuses. Can a desk clerk called Albert possibly be the father of the theory of relativity? Or a non-university-educated son of a glover be the world's greatest playwright? Surely not. That would make these people human, take the sheen off the lustre of their greatness, and stop them from being accessible only to the great and the good.

Not surprisingly then, considering this great point of discussion among Bard-lovers, one of the most frequent questions I get asked when people discover I'm into Shakespeare is: *Who do you think really wrote the plays?* My answer is always the same:

I don't care who *really* wrote Shakespeare's plays.

There are 39 plays and 154 sonnets ascribed to someone called Shakespeare. I'd be the first to admit that some of the writing isn't so hot, but most of it is absolutely jaw-droppingly, groundbreakingly breathtaking, I mean really, really quite brilliant, and the plays are what bake my cake, not so much the man and his life.

With 39 known plays and a collection of sonnets, Shakespeare may not be the most prolific Elizabethan writer (Thomas Heywood, a contemporary of Shakespeare's, claimed to have a hand in over 200 works), but his plays were loved then, and 400 years on, whoever he was, he is now generally considered to be the greatest writer of the English language.

Beyond that, most of everything else 'known' about him is speculation, so I'm not going to discuss whether his birth and death dates are actually the same, where he might have gone during his 'lost' years, where he lived in London, whether or not he ate toast, and whether or not he was Catholic or Protestant, gay or straight. No one knows any of these things about him for sure, and we probably never will, but there are plenty of fascinating books out there that try to guess.

If some part of Shakespeare's life is relevant, I'll mention it, but I say again, a good solid part of Shakespeare's life is a mystery to us. With the smattering of signatures and legal papers that we have, we actually know more about him than we do about many of his contemporaries, but that still isn't very much to go on. Perhaps 90 per cent of his life is shrouded in mystery.

See, I just used the word 'perhaps'. So much of this man is guesswork.

So instead, I'm going to concentrate on what Elizabethan life was like, what it would have been like going to the theatre in Shakespeare's time, how different an experience it would have been compared to our time, why Shakespeare wrote in poetry, and exactly why all of that is so very important in getting into his plays.

Scene 5

An Elizabethan theatre

While we may not know much about the man, we know quite a lot about the time he wrote in, and the plays themselves:

§ Incredibly, virtually every word he wrote was penned over the course of twenty years, from about 1590 to 1610, during which time there were some huge changes in Elizabethan society.

§ Queen Elizabeth I was on the throne until 1603, then King James VI of Scotland succeeded her, but the period is still usually referred to as *Elizabethan*.

§ Going to the theatre in Shakespeare's time was a very different experience from going to the theatre nowadays; it was probably more like a modern football match. We know from diaries of visitors to London that the theatres were rowdy, drunken places, so …

§ … there was no 'theatre etiquette' that made the audience sit or stand still quietly. That air of formality seems to have developed only in the last couple of hundred years.

§ In Elizabethan times, rarely would a play be repeated – rarely would you have the luxury of being able to see it twice – as there was usually a new play on every day. That never happens now …

§ … but even if a play was repeated, if you'd seen it once you wouldn't be likely to pay to see it again (see the box on page 20).

§ Consequently, the demand for new plays was, as you might imagine, huge. Everyone would be writing them, much like it seems everyone in Hollywood has written a screenplay. Thirty-nine of Shakespeare's plays have survived the last four centuries – more might well have been lost to time – but that still means he must have been writing at least a couple of new plays every year. (Compare that to modern playwrights, who might write and get a new play produced perhaps every two years or so.)

The plague (or the *Black Death*, to give its more fun title) hit London many times during Shakespeare's life. When it hit, the playhouses and theatres were closed – the disease was so contagious and the audiences were packed in so tightly that the theatres would have been a real breeding ground for the plague to spread – and the demand for new plays disappeared overnight.

How much did it cost to go to the theatre in Elizabethan times?

A typical wage in 1594 was 8 old pence a day; in Shakespeare's Globe you had the choice of several places to watch and hear a play.

- For a penny, you could stand in the yard around the stage, as a 'groundling'.

- For twopence, you could sit on a wooden seat in a covered gallery set out in a semi-circle around the yard. There were three tiers of galleries.

- For another penny, you could hire a cushion to make the seats a little more comfortable (despite the fleas).

- For sixpence, you could sit in the Lords' Gallery – seats placed at either side of the balcony at the back of the stage, which meant you were facing the audience, and looking down on the play from behind. Like the boxes of modern theatres, it was more for people who wanted to be seen rather than see.

Sunlit, rowdy, drunken, elaborately built places for the most part, the playhouses would have been a popular destination – a circular, hemmed-in, almost secret world away from the rest of the city – but more on this in Act 2 …

With the theatres closed, the theatre companies and the playwrights were out of work, and needing money (imagine the hordes of TV writers looking for work if TV was banned for two years …).

Theatre companies could make money by selling a printer manuscripts of the plays they'd performed, but printing was still a relatively new thing. William Caxton had brought the printing press to England only a hundred years beforehand, and the process was still fairly complicated. A page of text would be set using letter blocks, and it wasn't unknown for the printer to run out of blocks or space, so spellings would vary depending on how many *e*'s he had to hand, as well as how much space was left on the page. Once set, the page would be pressed, then the blocks would be broken up and used to make another page. It would have been a loooong process.

Copyright law was a little different back then, and it worked like this: once a playwright had finished writing, he'd sell his play (and its copyright) to the theatre company for performance. The theatre company could then make money by selling the play to the printer, but the playwright wouldn't see a single penny of that sale. Likewise, any money the printer made from sales of copies of that play would never be seen by the theatre company or the playwright.

In times of plague, with the theatres shut, selling plays to a printer was often a theatre company's *only* way of making money. Playwrights, however, were left with the option of either trying to print unused manuscripts of their own, or writing poetry. Or, unthinkable though it might be, getting a proper job.

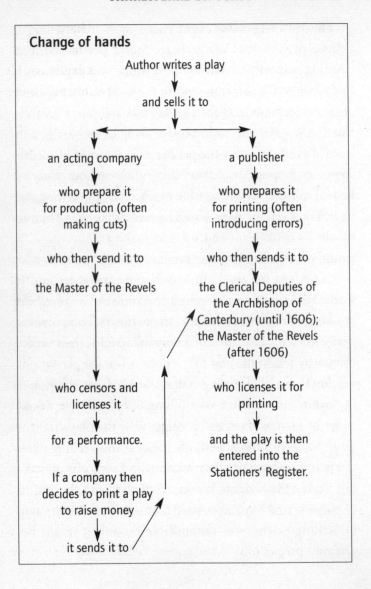

Change of hands

Author writes a play

and sells it to

an acting company

who prepare it
for production (often
making cuts)

who then send it to

the Master of the Revels

who censors and
licenses it

for a performance.

If a company then
decides to print a play
to raise money

it sends it to

a publisher

who prepares it
for printing (often
introducing errors)

who then sends it to

the Clerical Deputies of
the Archbishop of
Canterbury (until 1606);
the Master of the Revels
(after 1606)

who licenses it for
printing

and the play is then
entered into the
Stationers' Register.

Selling unused manuscripts would have been hard – selling copies of plays that *had* been performed was hard enough – as there just wasn't the demand. Paper was expensive, 80 per cent of Elizabethans couldn't read, and, after all, plays were written to be *performed*, not read.

The lack of demand, the loss of the copyright, and the fact that more fame and money would come from performance, meant that even during plague epidemics, writers in Elizabethan times weren't interested in having their plays printed – if there isn't any money in it, what's the point?

Shakespeare seems to have been no different. During the plague years of 1593–94, when work and money would have been scarce to non-existent, a couple of his plays were published in quarto (see box on page 25), but it appears that he spent most of his time concentrating on writing, rather than publishing.

In 1599, he became a shareholder of the newly built Globe Theatre, and so would have received 10 per cent of any profits the theatre made, including any monies from printing plays. There would have been bills to pay from the building of the new Globe too, but *still* no major printing of his works took place while he was alive.

Despite the fact that eighteen of his plays were published in quarto (mostly unofficially) during his lifetime, there's no record of Shakespeare being involved in their printing; indeed, many are thought to have been under-taken by rival companies, copying the plays down while watching them, and printing the results. They're often referred to as 'bad quartos', and they certainly vary greatly in quality. (Ben Jonson was the first playwright who took an interest in printing his own plays, and supervised the publication of his Works in 1616.)

For most of us, 400 years on, our first meeting with Shakespeare is in a book and on a page, which is ironic, as all evidence points towards the fact that this would be far from the way Elizabethan audiences would have received them – and more to the point, given that he didn't seem to want them printed, far from the way Shakespeare would have intended them to be received.

I like the idea that Shakespeare wasn't interested in hav-ing his plays printed. It makes sense. Nowadays we get caught up reading the plays and not watching them so much, something Shakespeare seems to have practically barred his audience from doing. Don't read my plays, come and see them!

The result of this printing reticence, though, is that we nearly lost them all to history. Original single publications of Shakespeare's plays are incredibly scarce, and no one yet has discovered a treasure chest of original manuscripts that Shakespeare locked away for safe-keeping.

Half of Shakespeare's plays, like many of those of his

contemporaries, might have disappeared entirely were it not for two of his actors who took it upon themselves to bring all his works together and print them. Seven years after Shakespeare died, they published a book called the *First Folio* – which became one of the most important books printed in theatre, literary, and linguistic history.

Folio or quarto?

A play would be printed on paper, which at the time was very expensive to make. To save money, a piece of paper would be either

- ₷ folded into quarters – these editions were known as quartos and were much cheaper to produce, and therefore to buy, as you'd get eight pages from one piece;

- ₷ or folded in half – these editions were known as folios and were more expensive, as you'd have only four sides to print on.

Plays weren't usually printed in folio, so for Shakespeare to have his plays collected in this way meant that people (a) felt his plays *were* ~~was~~ really rather good, and (b) were willing to fork out a fairly hefty sum for a copy, which may not have been the case when he was alive, but certainly seemed to be the case seven years after his death ...

If this little book hadn't been published in 1623, we would have lost eighteen of Shakespeare's plays – including *The Tempest, The Comedy of Errors, Macbeth* and *Twelfth Night*

– and, as the other eighteen were only scattered about in quarto, we might have lost them too (this count excludes the three plays that have been acknowledged in recent times as being written, at least in part, by Shakespeare: *Cymbeline*, *Edward III*, and *The Two Noble Kinsmen*).

Of the thousands of plays written over those times, only 230 are still in existence: 39 of them – 17 per cent – are Shakespeare's.

Henry Condell and John Hemmings had acted and worked with Shakespeare during much of his writing career, and they got together after Shakespeare died to set the record straight. Too many versions of his plays had been printed full of mistakes by rival theatre companies trying to steal Shakespeare's plays. There were quarto editions without Shakespeare's name on them, editions of *Hamlet* missing chunks of the text ... The new folio edition would address all that.

The (bad) First Quarto of *Hamlet* ...

This was written in 1603, probably from memory, and we should be thankful that Shakespeare's most famous speech didn't survive only in this incarnation:

To be, or not to be, I [ay] there's the point,
To Die, to sleepe, is that all? I all:

No, to sleepe, to dreame, I mary [marry] there it goes,
For in that dreame of death, when wee awake,
And borne before an euerlasting iudge,
From whence no passenger euer retur'nd,
The vndiscovered country, at whose sight
The happy smile, and the accursed damn'd ...

As opposed to the version known and loved by all:

To be, or not to be – that is the question;
Whether 'tis nobler in the mind to suffer
The slings and arrows of outrageous fortune
Or to take arms against a sea of troubles
And by opposing end them. To die, to sleep –
No more, and by a sleep to say we end
The heartache and the thousand natural shocks
That flesh is heir to. 'Tis a consummation
Devoutly to be wished. To die, to sleep –
To sleep – perchance to dream. Ay, there's the rub ...

There are three known editions of *Hamlet* – the First Quarto of 1603, the Second Quarto of 1604, and the Folio version. Other editions were published, but these are considered to be amalgamations of the first three. The First Quarto wasn't discovered until 1823, and while being shorter than the other two, it does include an entire scene and many interesting stage directions that the others don't have. When the editors of the First Folio came to *Hamlet*, it looks as if they used a combination of manuscript and Second Quarto. With so many versions, each so different from the other, determining the 'authentic' text of *Hamlet*, as Shakespeare intended, has proved somewhat difficult.

So now, thank goodness, we have the plays. We're able to watch and read them over and over and over. Not only can we read or see them performed as much as we like, we have the luxury of being able to come to them with over 200 years of study behind us.

I say 200 years rather than 400, because after the Puritan movement took Shakespeare and many other writers out of the common eye, he didn't really became popular again until the late 18th century, largely thanks to the actor David Garrick and his Stratford-upon-Avon festival – but more on this in Act 5. Still, 200 years of study is an awful lot, and by standing on the shoulders of giants, the depth of analysis we can now put Shakespeare's plays under is limitless.

But because we hold Shakespeare in such regard – as high art and important Literature – and scrutinise his plays so intensely, we forget that reading them is simply not the way they would have originally been received.

The Elizabethans would watch and listen to a play in the theatre, and then leave it behind at the end of the after-noon. It's easy for us to get hold of a copy of one of the plays. But if you were an Elizabethan lucky enough to have had an education and had learnt to read, the play-texts, already scarce in quantity, would have been relatively expensive.

After Shakespeare died, the publication of the First

How much bread is Shakespeare worth?

When the *Collected Works* was printed in 1623, the book would have been stitched together, but not normally bound (it wouldn't have had a leather cover). An unbound copy would have cost around 15 shillings, and you could get a bound copy for £1.

But, good question, how expensive was that in Shakespeare's time?

Somebody once worked out that the average cost of one of these books is equivalent to the price of 44 Elizabethan loaves of bread.

Using the same measure, we can see how the price goes up over the years. It became more and more valuable as Shakespeare became more and more popular, and had risen to the equivalent of 105 loaves in 1756; then a big jump to 900 by the 1790s, most likely due to David Garrick's revival of Shakespeare with his annual festival of Shakespeare; 5,000 loaves in the 1850s – and 96,000 by the beginning of the 20th century.

Today, the figures are astronomical. An edition of the Folio sold at auction for over $6 million in 2001. The cheapest loaf in my local supermarket is 20 pence. That's (approximately) 17 million loaves for a copy of the original edition today, against 44 loaves in the early 1600s.

Folio meant that his plays were more readily available than ever before. So, suppose you could read, and you *could* spare the equivalent of 44 loaves of bread and afford the book, you might well buy the Folio and read the plays to remind yourself of the performance you saw, as we would buy a copy of a film we like.

But would an Elizabethan have analysed the plays as we do now? (It's highly unlikely – would you analyse an episode of a soap opera?) They would have accepted them much more at face value, and we can learn a great deal by looking at Shakespeare's plays with more of an Elizabethan head on our shoulders.

The way we're used to receiving the plays, in classrooms and practically under a microscope, couldn't be further away from their experience.

A few Shakespeare-coined phrases, still very much in use today ...

all that glitters is not gold 'All that glisters is not gold/Often have you heard that told' – *The Merchant of Venice*, Act 2, Scene 7, line 65

as dead as a door nail 'If I do not leave you all as dead as a doornail, I pray god I may never eat grass more' – *Henry VI Part 2*, Act 4, Scene 10, line 38

blinking idiot 'What's here? The portrait of a blinking idiot' – *The Merchant of Venice*, Act 2, Scene 9, line 54

fair play 'O. 'tis fair play' – *Troilus and Cressida*, Act 5, Scene 3, line 43

into thin air 'These our actors,/As I foretold you, were all spirits, and/Are melted into air, into thin air' – *The Tempest*, Act 4, Scene 1, line 150

set teeth on edge 'I had rather hear a ... a dry wheel grate on the axle-tree,/And that would set my teeth nothing on edge/Nothing so much as mincing poetry' – *Henry IV Part 1*, Act 3, Scene 1, line 127

slept a wink 'Since I received command to do this business I have not slept one wink' – *Cymbeline*, Act 3, Scene 4, line 99

to thine own self be true 'This above all: to thine own self be true' – *Hamlet*, Act 1, Scene 3, line 78

tower of strength 'the King's name is a tower of strength' – *Richard III*, Act 5, Scene 3, line 12

too much of a good thing 'Can one desire too much of a good thing?' – *As You Like It*, Act 4, Scene 1, lines 112–13

Scene 6

A classroom

The last 200 years have seen Shakespeare go from being a largely forgotten Elizabethan poet to being voted Man of the Millennium (admittedly by a poll consisting solely of BBC Radio 4 listeners, but still …). He's the most referenced, the most cross-referenced, the most analysed, the most written about, the most performed and the best-known man to grace the planet, religious figures aside.

And with that fame has come a respect, a trend to deify him, to make his plays sacrosanct. The six official commandments of Shakespeare:

You Cannot Change Any Of The Words
He Must Not Be Translated
He Must Be Performed A Certain Way
He Must Be Spoken A Certain Way
He Must Be Spoken Of In A Certain Way
We Will Celebrate His Birthday As If He Were Royalty

Alright, I just made those up. But you'd be surprised how many people deem every word absolute truth. And he's just a playwright. Or is he now a literary messiah?

I know now why I used to hate Shakespeare so much. It was this kind of 'holier than thou' opinion, compounded with the approach to teaching Shakespeare that is still prevalent: sitting down, reading or writing about the plays, or speaking them out loud without really knowing what it is that you're saying ... It takes them so completely out of context. It's like trying to appreciate the fun of driving a car or flying a plane by reading the engine's instruction manual.

My Gran tells me her Shakespeare classes were like that in her day, and 60 years on, she still doesn't understand Shakespeare. Who can blame her? But when you do see Shakespeare on stage and acted, something changes.

> *You read Shakespeare in school and you think it's rather boring as a rule. It's a lot of words ... But when you take the parts and act it ... then you begin to realise how interesting it is. And you realise how natural it is and how real. It doesn't seem like that when you read it.*

> June Brown, who plays *EastEnders*' Dot Cotton

Of *course* Shakespeare will seem out of reach when his plays are presented so clearly out of context. It's stating the obvious, but too many people forget that at the end of the day, Shakespeare was just a man. He ate, he drank, he had sex, he laughed, he pissed, he cried, he woke up hungover, he wrote, he ran out of ideas.

You might have seen the film *Shakespeare in Love* (1998). One of the greatest, smallest details in that film was that Joseph Fiennes (playing Will Shakespeare) had ink-stained, dirty fingernails. Using a feather quill and ink all the time would make that happen. That little detail spoke volumes to me. If Shakespeare got dirty, then he was human. If he was human, and not just some genius literary figure, then I can relate to him, and give his writing a chance.

It's unlikely that when he wrote, he sat down and thought: 'Today, I shall write a masterpiece so great that in 400 years' time they shall hang laurels around statues of me, and actors shall queue up to play my characters.' Possible, I admit, but unlikely.

He would have done what we all do. Panicked when he ran out of money. Rewrote old pieces in new ways. It was his job, but he had theatre in his blood too, and I think he *had* to write because it burned within him; there was a fiery passion for writing, combined with an earthy basic human need to earn money to live.

I want to be clear: he was a genius. But part of the problem with the label 'genius' is that it's unobtainable to anyone that isn't one. How can we normal folk relate to a genius? It's a hard concept to grapple with, and it gives rise to doubt and suspicion. William Shakespeare *can't* have written all those wonderful plays. He doesn't have the 'right' background or education. It *must* have been someone else writing them.

But he was human, and real, and bloody clever. Just like Einstein – who drank, partied, wore shabby clothes and worried about wars – was human. And Shakespeare didn't write so that 379 years after his death people would be preserving his works in vacuum-sealed bags and I'd be sitting in an exam hall trying to explain the existentialist viewpoint in his plays.

It comes down to this: if he didn't write good plays, he wouldn't earn any money. If he didn't earn any money, he wouldn't be able to support the wife and kids back in Stratford. He'd be put in the debtors' prison, and probably die a very horrible, cold death.

That's quite an incentive to do well.

So he wrote plays because there was a solid need for them; less that he sought fame, more that they were a real source of cash.

Much like the soap opera writers of today.

The Elizabethan stage fulfilled some of the same functions that soaps do today … the things that Shakespeare achieved are what script editors and storyliners on the soaps are also trying to achieve.

Michael Boyd, artistic director of the
Royal Shakespeare Company

Scene 7

A soap opera set

Many of Shakespeare's plays are based on famous stories that most Elizabethans already knew – and they would have enjoyed the retelling of these familiar stories immensely. They would have enjoyed Shakespeare's presentation of the fall of Troy (in *Troilus and Cressida*) much as we do when a film is made of a famous story well known to us, like *Titanic* (1997).

But, just like when we go to the cinema, it's doubtful the Elizabethans would have felt the need to watch the play again, or analyse its deeper meaning because they didn't understand bits of it. Now, go to see a film by the brilliant but somewhat surrealist film-director David Lynch and your brain might try to sneak out of your ear if you try to work out the plot.

Shakespeare was essentially providing the Elizabethans with their daily soap opera, and would you ever sit down with a script of *EastEnders, Coronation Street, Neighbours* or *Days of Our Lives*, and analyse the deeper meaning? Try to work out whether or not Pat really does love Frank, or whether Scott really was faithful to Charlene? (I'm showing my age with these plotlines, but you get the idea ...)

No, if there's something you missed, or you don't understand the scripts, you watch the omnibus at the weekend. But what's not to understand? It's well known, at least on *EastEnders* and *Corrie*, that the storylines over the years are essentially the same, they just feature different families, who all gather in the same pub (saving the producers money on locations). It's love and hate and sex and death and betrayal and friendship and lies and abuse. Shakespeare's the same.

It wouldn't be true to say that because the Elizabethans didn't have to work at Shakespeare, we don't have to either. Even ignoring the poetry angle, there's still 400 years of cultural divide separating us. But he's a lot closer to us than we might think.

There's not, if you start to think about it, that much difference between the plot of an episode of *'Enders* and the plot of, say, *Macbeth*. Love, hate. Sex, death. Betrayal, friendship.

We know that life, though – *real* life – no matter what the papers or the soap operas say, doesn't go from murder to betrayal to death to murder again, a bit of incest, and finish up with a spot more murder before tea.

Life, for most of us, is fairly normal. Most of us (luckily) don't have to deal with such huge matters every day. Soap operas, though, pile on these kinds of terrible life-changing events, one on top of the other, to keep us watching. The makers want to keep us involved, to heighten the drama as much as possible and make sure there's a cliff-hanger at the end of every episode to make us tune in next week.

This kind of writing has been going on for centuries: Charles Dickens wrote the chapters of his novels for a monthly magazine, so his stories are usually very long (the longer the story, the more issues to write for) and they often have a cliff-hanger at the end of each chapter. Keep reading. Buy more. Keep writing. Earn more.

The thriller writer Ken Follett follows the same theory – making sure there's a mini-drama, or 'story turn', as he calls it, every five pages or so:

> There is a rule which says that the story should turn about every four to six pages. A story turn is anything that changes the basic dramatic situation. You can't go longer than about six pages without a story turn, otherwise the reader will get bored. Although that is a rule that people have invented in modern times about best-sellers … in Dickens it's the same. Ken Follett

For the most part (hopefully), none of us will have experienced even a small amount of the pain and suffering we see taking place in these dramas. But there'll be *something* in it, *some* part of it that will touch some part of us, to make us say 'Yes, I've been there, yes, I've felt that.'

Shakespeare and soap operas

Sounds unlikely ... But in 2001 a survey commissioned by the Royal Shakespeare Company asked members of the public what were the modern equivalents to Shakespeare's history plays. *Coronation Street* and *EastEnders* came out on top of the list. And in August 2006 an edition of the TV magazine *Radio Times* proclaimed 'Why the soaps owe it all to Shakespeare!'

Kate Harwood, an executive producer on *EastEnders*, said: 'All drama nowadays owes something to Shakespeare.' She believes Shakespeare is responsible for the 'extraordinary, heart-stopping sense of moment' that soap operas try to have at the end of every episode, right before the music kicks in, 'when the story all hangs in the air, ripe with potential'.

If writers portrayed life as it really was, with all its silences and normal events – like the TV show *Big Brother Live* – we'd die of boredom (or exhaustion). Moreover, if we daily experienced what the characters in *EastEnders* go through, the LAST thing we'd want to do is watch someone go through the exact same thing.

But an idea of it, or something close to what we've been through, is comforting. It's good to know that there are people out there going through similar circumstances to us, that we're not alone in our problems, in our pain, in our happiness. Or, for that matter, to put it another way,

> It easeth some, though none it ever cured
> To think their dolour others have endured.

A favourite quote of mine, from one of Shakespeare's poems, *The Rape of Lucrece* (lines 1581–2. 'Dolour' means *grief*, or *sorrow*).

In intense situations in real life, most people don't swear every second word, break down and cry every two minutes; they don't have heart-breaking monologues. Most people pause and stutter and forget what they're saying.

But that isn't *dramatic*. That's normal. And why pay a penny to go stand in the mud and see three hours of people being *normal* to each other? Even modern plays that claim to be showing 'real life' are still giving a dramatic version of normality.

Similar to soap opera plot lines, Shakespeare's stories are far more dramatic than real life; and they would have been quite unlike anything an average Elizabethan audience might experience. But they would always find *something* in the plays to relate to.

Shakespeare is famous for putting the familiar next to the unfamiliar – the betrayal of a father next to the betrayal of a king. His stories manage to stay real and human, while at the same time exploring the very extremes of life, and the lengths humans will go to to get what they want. Very rarely do you find Shakespeare's characters doing 'regular' things; he didn't seem to be very interested in so-called 'kitchen-sink' drama. The characters were often ordinary folk, but the situations they found themselves in were usually quite extraordinary.

More often than not in drama, people want to see life and situations they'll *never* experience, either because it's harsher than real life (like *EastEnders*) or it looks at a more unobtainable style of life – like *Friends*, or *The OC* – aspirational drama that makes us want to experience what the characters are going through, if only for a moment.

We want to see what it's like to fall in love with your best friend's girlfriend. We want to know what it's like when all your friends are using you, and then, when you need them the most, they turn their back on you. We want to hear what it feels like to kill the person you love more than the world, and then try to live with the consequences.

We want, in other words, to see *The Two Gentlemen of Verona, Timon of Athens,* and *Othello.*

Acts and Scenes

Shakespeare's plays are now all divided up using the same convention, although they weren't all separated this way in the First Folio. It's thought that the plays which are divided into separate Acts were originally performed indoors, giving interval time for the chandeliers to be lowered and the candles replaced, and those without divisions were performed in daylight, and so needed no forced break.

But all modern editions are based on the classical Latin system of writing plays that Shakespeare would have studied at school: there are always five Acts, and in his plays, each Act has anything from one to fifteen Scenes.

Over the years they've been referred to in different ways, and depending on which edition of the plays you go to, you'll come across a variety of conventions:

§ Latin was used in the First Folio – Actus Primus, Scoena Prima for Act 1, Scene 1, and the lines were not numbered.

§ Editions from the 20th century added line numbers every five or ten lines to the side of the text, to make it easier to reference particular parts. Many would also name the Acts and Scenes using Roman numerals. So *Romeo and Juliet IV.iii.58* would take you to Act 4, Scene 3, line 58.

§ People use Roman numerals less and less nowadays, preferring a more concise *RJ 4.3.58*. There are too many differing abbreviations of the play-names to list them all, like *Rom* or *RJ* for *Romeo and Juliet*, but fortunately most are fairly straightforward.

Act 2

Curtain Up

Scene 1

Mars, 23rd century

The Elizabethans watching one of Shakespeare's plays would be relatively unaccustomed to seeing pictures or images – save perhaps a sign outside a tavern, a portrait or tapestry.

In our time, unless you make an incredible effort, it's impossible to turn a corner without seeing a photograph or the printed word – our streets and homes are littered with them. But very few Elizabethans would have been able to afford the equivalent distractions for their homes – tapestries, sculptures, woodcuttings or paintings – and as only 20 per cent of them could read, few might discover the images printed in books.

Our love for images has become insatiable, and in our media-rich 21st-century world we're quite used to seeing people dressed up, pretending to be someone they're not. Our ability to believe in something fictional – our suspension of disbelief – has been working well since childhood, thanks to the marvels of TV and film.

From the age of four, we all know that everyone on screen is pretending; that the spaceship is a model, that the

*dinosaur is CGI. And we love the double-think; the
mental game we play with ourselves, wondering how they
do it, while at the same time feeling a quickening of the
pulse and a tightening of the throat as the tension mounts.*

playwright Mark Ravenhill, writing in *The Guardian*,
November 2006

The greatest effort is made (and millions of dollars are
spent) to bring the unbelievable before our eyes – all is
provided for us, either on screen and the internet, or with
painted backdrops, from the canals of Venice to life on
Mars in the 23rd century. Elizabethans would have had to
imagine the magician Prospero's island in *The Tempest*. We
can digitally create one that we know is fake, but are willing
to believe in anyway (as long as it meets our increasingly
high standards). The point is that while our suspension of
disbelief is working well, our imaginations have become
lazy. Unless we're reading a novel, our imaginations might
as well be surgically removed these days. But who needs to
read the book, when the film comes out next year?

To help our increasingly busy minds, most theatres and
cinemas drop the lights when the show starts. In theatres
this really is a relatively recent phenomenon – about 200
years ago, the audiences in indoor theatres would be as
well lit as the actors. But now, for the most part, we sit in a

dark room, and the only source of light – and so the only real focus – is the play or film.

Perhaps this is more useful to a modern audience, as the forced focus makes it easier to forget our knowledge of celebrity casting and computer-generated images, and lets us slip into the fabricated world more quickly; but a glance at a fire exit light or a ring of a mobile phone will bring us out of it just as rapidly.

Visit the Globe today, where the actors and audience are equally lit, where helicopters regularly fly overhead, and it can be hard to forget the modern world. But then why go to the theatre and imagine a boat sailing across a sea, when we can go to the cinema and see it 'for real'?

Lazy imaginations make producing 400-year-old plays that much harder, because who, in this day and age, is afraid of witches any more?

We're a tougher, more critical audience to win over, needing better tricks and more believable effects to dupe us.

Believable?

During the American Civil War (1861–65) a soldier watching a performance of *Othello* was so taken in by the actor playing the dishonest Iago that he stood up from his seat, drew his pistol and shot the actor dead.

So without the internet, films, television, magazines, and everything else we have at our fingertips available to them, Shakespeare's audience had an exceptionally open and hungry imagination. They were an audience that would love fabulous, exotic worlds being weaved before them, worlds they'd never experience, people wearing clothes they'd never wear, saying things they themselves would perhaps never get to say.

So that's what Shakespeare gave them.

He'd hear stories of far-off lands, and write plays about them. Imagine! A city of canals …

Like his contemporaries, he would rewrite classic stories that everyone knew. Imagine! Seeing the Battle of Agincourt, the fall of Troy and the beauty of Helen, stories you've known backwards since you were a child …

> Work, work your thoughts, and therein see a siege
> > *(Henry V*, Act 3, line 25 of the Chorus)

Just use your imagination, he says, and see the battle before you.

There had to be a balance, though, if your audience believed so wholly in what they saw: some things reminding you it's not real, and some keeping you firmly in the bubble of the world being weaved before you. It had to be entertaining and believable *and* yet clearly not real: you didn't want your audience starting to riot whenever a character was killed.

Even we can still have problems remembering what's real and what's not: when actors have been playing the same parts for years, the line between the actor and the part they play often seems to become blurred. How different are the actors in *Friends* from the characters they play? An actor friend of mine played a villain in *Dream Team* (a football soap on satellite TV), and was regularly shouted at by random members of the public. They thought that because his character was a bad guy, then he must be too.

That blurring of lines comes much *closer* to the way Elizabethans would have seen the action on stage 400 years ago. Their ability to wholly believe in what they were watching would have been far greater than ours is now. Very little would have been handed to them, in a visual sense. Little or no set, sound effects, or lighting to help their imaginations along. You had to work with what was in front of you, because that's all there was – so if you saw it with your own eyes it *must* be true. If you saw someone die on stage, then that person was *dead*!

Theatres in Shakespeare's time were a tough place to hold an audience's attention, even ones with vital, active imaginations. They were rowdy, drunken places, and were used only in broad daylight (indoor theatres could use candles, but they gave poor light and were expensive), so no darkened room with a lit stage to draw the focus.

But still, within these raucous, wooden spaces, filled with beer sellers and prostitutes, lords and commoners, magical, fantastical worlds were being weaved.

Scene 2

The Globe, Bankside, 17th century

THE STAGE

The space that Shakespeare's plays were performed in is important. Now we have the reconstructed Shakespeare's Globe in London, we can get as close as possible to Shakespeare's working home, and the birthplace of these seemingly inaccessible plays.

Some consider the Globe to be nothing more than a tourist spot. It's not. We've learnt so much about how to perform Shakespeare's plays in the reconstructed Globe in the last ten years, finally getting to act them in the type of space they were originally written for.

The bulk of the plays were presented in the Globe Theatre: a round, wooden building, with an open roof. I'm going to use the Globe as the main example, as it was also the theatre Shakespeare had a financial stake in. There were a number of other outdoor theatres, and quite a few indoor theatres too, not to mention non-theatrical spaces like the Middle Temple and the Court, but the Globe (and its modern counterpart) is the most accessible of the original playing spaces.

At the Globe, a very large part of the audience would be standing almost entirely around the stage in the yard. There were three galleries above the yard, and the people in the galleries would be sitting – if you imagine a clock face, from 8 o'clock through 4 o'clock – with the actors standing at the centre.

A view from the audience to the stage at Shakespeare's Globe, London, by Jim Alexander.

The stage would be raised up from the ground, perhaps to waist height, perhaps higher (we don't know for sure), so the actors were clearly separated from the audience.

There would have been a roof over the stage, supported by two pillars; a balcony above the stage, and doors at the back for exits and entrances.

As the plays would have been performed during the afternoon (there being no practical way to light the theatre at night), the actors would have seen every member of the audience.

That's such an important point that I want to switch perspective for a second. I've acted at the reconstructed Globe in London, and you quickly discover how much of a thrill it is to see the faces of 1,500 people while acting Shakespeare. It means you can speak these personal, passionate speeches directly to one person, if you want. And another part of the speech to a completely different person.

But the magic begins to really spark when the people sitting or standing around the person you're looking at think you're looking directly at them too, and so in groups of twenty or so at a time, parts of the audience feel as if a moment of the play is for them and them alone.

Is this unusual? Well, actually, yes it is, when you think that for the last couple of hundred years Shakespeare's lines have mostly been delivered by actors to audiences sitting in the dark, and as far as the actor is concerned there could be 500 people watching or there could be five.

At the Globe an actor can see if the audience are enjoying themselves, if they're cold, wet, happy or sad, bored or laughing, talking, crying or on their mobile phones, and this brings a connection between you that can't be found anywhere else.

The audience can affect the actors, too...

In a recent production of *The Comedy of Errors* at Shakespeare's Globe in London, the actors playing Dromio and Antipholus of Syracuse sat at one of the pillars and chatted (in Act 2, Scene 2).

When Dromio says 'There's no time for a man to recover his hair that grows bald by nature', he saw a bald man in the audience and pointed at him. The audience fell about. Then, a little later, Dromio says 'There's many a man who has more hair than wit', so the actor pointed to a particularly hairy man, and again the audience fell about.

Act or watch Shakespeare in as original a setting as possible, like at the Globe, and every show will make you reconsider and find a new meaning to lines you thought you'd always totally understood.

This actor–audience joint experience would have been going on (mobile phones aside) in a very similar way in Shakespeare's time, if not more so. When *Henry V* was performed at the reconstructed Globe, the audience began to cheer the English army, and boo the French; and in most shows there, audiences clap along with the rhythm of the songs and dances, though it can be slightly hesitant, as we modern audiences are so used to sitting quietly and behaving.

Modern audiences heckle comedians in stand-up shows, where there is less etiquette in behaving. Globe audiences sometimes heckle the actors, too, when they're feeling brave. The Elizabethans would have had no reason, no etiquette, to stop them from heckling, shouting, throwing things at the actors, either in appreciation or disapproval.

Back to the stage. We know there probably wouldn't have been a set, as we would think of it – no flat pieces of wood with pictures of rooms, or countryside background drawn on, to establish 'where' a particular scene is set – the words would do that, with the actors bringing on odd pieces (flasks, weapons or cushions) to help place the scenes. The theatre, in all its massive glory, was the set.

So irrespective of whether the theatre was gaily coloured or not, what we have is a very simple open space, in a big, grand, solid wooden building – and this was the bare minimum needed to tell Shakespeare's stories.

The single biggest clue we have about the inside of the space is from the opening Chorus speech from *Henry V* – though, as I've already said in relation to the man himself, taking historical fact from Shakespeare's writing is a dangerous path to wander down, and should be issued with a pinch of salt:

> But pardon, gentles all,
> The flat unraisèd spirits that have dared
> On this unworthy scaffold to bring forth
> So great an object. Can this cockpit hold
> The vasty fields of France? Or may we cram
> Within this wooden O the very casques
> That did affright the air at Agincourt?
> O, pardon! since a crookèd figure may
> Attest in little place a million,
> And let us, ciphers to this great account,
> On your imaginary forces work.

He's saying: 'Excuse, everyone, these awful actors who dare to perform such a wonderful spectacle in this terrible space (*scaffold*). Can this tiny place (*cockpit*) hold the enormous countryside of France? Or the ferocious soldiers (*casques*) who fought at the battle of Agincourt? Do forgive us, because one poor actor is going to represent a million. And let us, most unworthy nothings (*ciphers*), work on your imagination ...'

In this awful space, this 'wooden O' shape, let us help your imaginations: the implication is that there's nothing else, no legions of soldiers, no pictures of trees, no set to help your imagination create the scenes before you, nothing other than the actors.

People were said to go and *hear*, or *audit*, a play (hence *audience*), not to go and see a play. In fact, because of the pillars supporting the roof over the stage, it's unlikely that any one member of the audience could see everything that happened all of the time on stage. At the reconstructed Globe this is absolutely the case – there's no one point when you act on the stage where you can be seen by all the audience, so the pillars make you, ask you, almost *beg* you to walk around them so all the audience get at least a glimpse of you.

The rowdy audience of Shakespeare's time may have made it hard for the actors to be heard too, but the omnipresence of the pillars does imply that *seeing* what was happening was not as important as *hearing* what was being said.

The words, said aloud and spoken with feeling, conjured fantasies and images, ships and storms, houses and forests out of the air and into the greedy minds of the audience.

The Chorus

The character of the Chorus is similar to a narrator, who speaks directly to the audience. He often sets the scene, tells the audience if the action has moved to a different country, or describes moments that have taken place that they're not going to see. At the end of *Henry V*, the Chorus apologises for the poor quality of the writing – *with rough and all-unable pen* – and it was quite normal for him to apologise so profusely, very much a case of false modesty; so his apology for the poor state of the theatre in the opening of *Henry V* could equally just be mock humility.

Did Elizabethan actors rehearse?

There's a very good chance they didn't – mainly due to a lack of time. The theatre manager Philip Henslowe records in his diary that there would have been a performance of a new play most days of the week, and, as we've seen, the same play was rarely performed twice in one week. This means that Shakespeare's actors would probably have had 20–30 plays rattling around their heads at any one time.

At one point Henslowe noted that there were 23 plays being performed by the same group of actors. With all that learning of lines, would there have been time to rehearse?

Here's an idea of *A Day in the Life of an Elizabethan Actor* ...

- Wake at dawn, eat breakfast, get to the theatre;

- Learn and run through any fights or dances needed. Check you have all your props and costume;

- Perform around 2 o'clock in the afternoon;

- Get your role and scroll for the play to be performed tomorrow;

- Find your props and costume for that play, and learn (or finish off learning) your scroll. Ensure that this is done by nightfall, because the poor-quality smoky candles afforded by actors would make it difficult or impossible to do any reading at home;

- Visit an ale tavern (some things don't change);

- To bed, then the same again.

If they didn't rehearse, then they didn't have a director – though we'll see how Shakespeare managed to direct them himself through the lines he gave them, in Act 5.

The Costumes

Let's recap for a moment.

We have the plays, being spoken in an uncluttered (because of the lack of set) but rather unique space. There's a fair degree of distraction, with the crowd talking and jeering, which means there's not a great deal to help us into this imagined world. Still, all our imaginative energy is focused on this raised platform, and on these actors telling us a story.

Keeping our distracted minds on the stage and on the story would have been tricky for any actor, but they would have had a little help: one thing we know for sure is that a great deal of money was spent on their costumes.

How much did a costume cost?

Thanks to the diary of the theatre manager Philip Henslowe (c. 1550–1616), we have an idea of how much money was put towards the costumes.

He notes that he bought 'a black velvet cloak with sleeves embroidered all with silver and gold' for £20 10s 6d.

That would be equivalent to £2,692 today, or 1,642 Elizabethan loaves of bread, or more than a third of the price Shakespeare paid for the finest house in Stratford ...

So actors dress in the most fantastic costumes money can buy to look fabulous, give the audience something pretty to look at, and, after all, show they're playing a character: if the actors were to dress the same way as ordinary folk, how would we know when they were being *them*, and when they were being the character – like a murderer? If I'm wandering down an Elizabethan backstreet after I've seen the play *Macbeth*, and I see the actor who played the Second Murderer walking towards me and he's wearing the same clothes as he was on stage, does that mean he's actually a killer, and I should turn and walk the other way in case he kills me?

Or, turn the tables: an actor who played the villain leaves the theatre still in his costume, and is attacked by a mob who wanted the hero to win. It wouldn't be too hard to imagine, especially after hearing the 19th-century anecdote of the soldier shooting the actor playing Iago. My friend from *Dream Team* experienced something akin to that inability to separate truth from fiction, and the media practically encourages it – soap opera actors feature on the cover of TV magazines, and underneath their pictures the headlines usually refer to them using their character names rather than their real names, further blurring the line between real life and drama.

The unspoken rule even today is never to leave the theatre with your costume and your make-up on. It's considered unlucky to do so.

A slightly more practical and obvious danger to the

Elizabethan actors would be the wrath of a theatre manager like Philip Henslowe, who heavily fined his actors if they were late or if their costumes were damaged and needed repair. The vast expense of the costumes meant that they'd be especially careful not to walk the streets wearing them, in case they got torn or dirtied.

Costumes they wore, and cheap they were not. They were certainly beautiful, crafted with care, and were an important ingredient in creating a spectacle, keeping this magical bubble of the play's world from bursting.

THE JIG

Then, at the end of a performance, just as the world had been so carefully created, the breaking of the spell was just as considered.

At the end of every show, whether it was a comedy or a tragedy, there would be a dance, or jig. The jig is a brilliantly simple device and the modern Globe uses it in its productions. The idea is that if everyone gets up and starts dancing merrily together – hero and villain, dead man and live man – then everything *must* be okay, so go home safe and happy. Whatever magic, fantasy, terrible torment, viciousness or frivolity had been witnessed, is now well and truly over.

More emphatic than a simple bow or curtsy, the jig is a

celebratory affirmation of the story that has been told and the emotional journey the actors and audience have shared, and a fantastic release of tension.

It's bloody good fun too.

Scene 3

A galaxy far, far away

Take an incredible space, fill it with an audience with hungry imaginations, and you need great stories too.

A neuro-psychologist friend of mine told me that he thinks *Othello* is the greatest study of jealousy ever made, better than any research or medical paper he'd come across. Many people think *Romeo and Juliet* is the most romantic tale ever told. *Titus Andronicus* is definitely one of the bloodiest plays I've ever seen, and *King Lear* is easily one of the most heartbreaking.

But the stories Shakespeare told need putting into context a little.

He was telling stories before Dickens. Before Hemingway, Joyce, Twain, Austen, the Brontë sisters, the Brothers Grimm, and Milton's *Paradise Lost*.

This boggles me a little bit. What did he have to inspire him?

We, telling stories in the 21st century, can look back admiringly over the last few hundred years at the stories that have been conjured up for us. We have stories we've known since childhood, like *Little Red Riding Hood* and *Rapunzel*, and Hans Christian Andersen's fairy tales of *The*

Ugly Duckling and *The Princess and The Pea.* Then we had the work from all these other great authors to read (or I suppose, in recent times, to see the film versions of) when we were growing up. So when it comes to writing these days, new authors have so much to inspire them.

None of these tales existed when Shakespeare was writing. He had such very different stories available to him. As ever, we'll never know exactly what he read, but it seems clear that he was familiar with historical sources like Raphael Holinshed's *Chronicles*, and Thomas North's translation of Plutarch. The Latin authors Ovid and Horace, and Aesop's *Fables*, would have been around too. Not to forget the Bible, the Book of Common Prayer, Dante's *Inferno*, and Chaucer's *Troilus and Criseyde* and *The Canterbury Tales*.

Many of the books that were around to influence Shakespeare are almost out of our memory, yet the stories he dreamt up will be familiar to us, because they've influenced the writers who follow him. Before Robinson Crusoe was stuck on his island, Prospero the magician was shipwrecked. Before Pip's Great Expectations, there were tales of Pericles' life and love. Long before Superman and the Incredible Hulk, Hercules and Achilles walked the earth.

Shakespeare wrote about cruel kings, famous battles, love lost and won, children losing parents, parents losing children – universal themes that are so pervasive, so intrinsically known to us all that they can still work when they're adapted for TV and film. Whether a play is set in Elizabethan times or in an American high school (Tim Blake Nelson's 2001 adaptation of *Othello*, *O*, is a good example of the latter), the stories are both so general and so specific that they can handle almost any reworking. (Though they may not technically be Shakespeare any more, as the poetry is often first to go in these reworkings.)

Most of the original ideas were not Shakespeare's creations. Rewriting old stories was common practice, and he certainly wasn't the only one in his time who wrote new versions of classics. He was by no means alone in retelling the story of *Romeo and Juliet*, or *Troilus and Cressida*, or the *Reign of Henry V*. The Elizabethans would have known the stories that Shakespeare used as the basis for his plays. Copies of some of the originals have survived, so we know, for instance, that *Hamlet* was part-inspired by the 13th-century *Life of Amleth*. Originality was not the prerequisite for being a popular writer – the Elizabethans wanted the stories they'd heard since childhood, of evil kings and fated lovers, told and retold over and over.

We're very similar in that respect, and it still happens a lot today. The film *Star Wars* (1977) is based on a bunch of different old Japanese stories. Classic films are remade constantly (whether for better or worse). Many of the soap operas on TV have been running so long they often use plot lines from their own old episodes.

So if everyone was doing it back then (and writers are still doing it), why were Shakespeare's plays more popular? Why have his endured, and no one seems to have come close to topple his success? Why haven't the plays of one of his contemporaries like Henry Chettle (c. 1560–1607) been turned into films? Why have just a few of his contemporaries found only relative fame, like John Webster (c. 1580–1632)? If his audience knew the stories so well, what made them go to see Shakespeare's plays more than anyone else's?

It ain't what you say, it's the way that you say it …

Scene 4

A room full of character

Many people hold that the main reason why Shakespeare has become so universally thought of as just plain brilliant is because of the characters he wrote. It wouldn't be *my* first reason (which we're coming to), but without doubt, he had a way of creating memorable and pretty fantastic characters that make most other writers' creations seem amateur.

In *Henry IV Parts 1* and *2*, he wrote a character called Falstaff – a drunken, cowardly buffoon of a knight, who had become friends with the young Prince Hal. His relationship with Hal is beautifully tragic; and the scrapes Falstaff gets into are incredibly funny. Falstaff dies in *Henry V*, but the story goes that Queen Elizabeth I was such a fan of the character that she asked Shakespeare to bring him back and write another play with him in. And so he did, and so we have the romp that is *The Merry Wives of Windsor*.

A similar thing happened to Sir Arthur Conan Doyle, when he killed off his great detective character Sherlock Holmes. There was a public outcry, and he had to bring him back. Philip Pullman, author of the *His Dark Materials* trilogy, published a novella in 2008 called *Once*

Upon a Time in the North, which precedes the events of the *Dark Materials* and features two of the favourite characters who'd been killed off in the original stories. It happens with soap operas too, with Bobby in *Dallas*, Harold in *Neighbours*, and Dirty Den in *EastEnders* all being brought back 'from the dead', usually with an 'amnesiac' storyline or a wave of hocus-pocus writing.

While his characters are often great, Shakespeare is not the man to go to for a history lesson. Not an accurate one, anyway.

The Richard III Society was founded in 1924 because there was a growing group of people who were upset that Shakespeare had misrepresented King Richard III; claiming that he was a good king, and not an evil, murderous tyrant. Shakespeare based his play *Richard III* on Thomas More's *History of Richard III*, but the Society argues that More biased his account, including giving Richard a hunchback and making him appear more evil than he actually was. Their argument follows that More's rewriting of history meant that the monarch of the time, Henry VII (who deposed Richard), had a stronger claim to the throne.

Whether Richard III actually was a good person in real life is up for discussion. What cannot be disputed is that a troubled, evil tyrant-with-a-hunch makes a more dramatic, intriguing character to watch in the theatre. Troubled-tyrant-with-a-hunch rather than good person, every time.

Keeping good company ...

We're unlikely to ever know the specifics of their relationships, but Shakespeare's company of players (known as *The Lord Chamberlain's Men* in the reign of Elizabeth I, and *The King's Men* in the reign of James I) was one of the two leading theatre companies in London in the late 16th/early 17th centuries. Having the reigning monarch as patron to your company – and indeed, then having that patronage continued by the new monarch – was a very worthy, useful and honourable position to be in.

Forever remaining debatable is the influence of the monarchs on Shakespeare's writing, though, as I've said, it seems Elizabeth was influential in the arrival (around 1597) of *The Merry Wives of Windsor*, and, as we'll see later, it would be hard to see how the ascension of the Scots King James VI to the English throne in 1603 isn't somehow reflected in *Macbeth* (written around 1605).

It's thought that some lines from *Hamlet* (around 1601) were removed from an early quarto – either by Shakespeare or the Master of the Revels (who licensed and censored the plays) – to avoid offending Anne of Denmark, James's queen. The Office of the Master of the Revels' aim was to keep the monarch amused and not offended, and their mandate was censorship, not suppression. It's possible to see evidence of the Master of the Revels' censoring in the manuscript of *Sir Thomas More*, a play thought to have been written in part by Shakespeare.

Of course, Shakespeare's Richard III is an invention to some extent, just as his Henry V and Macbeth characters are. They'll have been based on the original kings, but end up as an amalgamation of characters and stories that

Shakespeare would have heard, letting his instincts as a dramatist choose the right bits to make the best heroes and villains.

The side effect of this skilful dramatic manipulation is the power Shakespeare was unwittingly wielding: establishing a great, fictional image who becomes far better-known than the real historical figure. That's quite some power.

Not only are the characters fascinating, the journeys they go on are equally powerful. In the very first scene of *Titus Andronicus*, the returning general Titus sacrifices the captured Goth Queen's son, and then, in a fit of anger, kills one of his own sons. Later in the play, his daughter is raped, her hands and tongue cut off. By the end of the first half, all but one of Titus' sons is killed. He then finds a way to get revenge, in a brilliantly bloody way, culminating in the Goth Queen feasting on a pie, baked by Titus, made of her sons' flesh and bones. It's a terrific journey for a character.

Hamlet, probably the most famous of all Shakespeare's characters, is mourning his father's death. A ghost appears, claiming to be the spirit of his father, also claiming that Hamlet's uncle Claudius, who has recently married Hamlet's mother, murdered him. Should Hamlet believe the ghost and take his revenge? Or, as was thought at the time, could the ghost be the devil in disguise, trying to tempt him to evil?

These are massive, extraordinarily complex characters, and there are hundreds more. For every one of these characters, someone from every different culture in every country in the world brings a fresh interpretation to the part, creating the play anew, because no matter where they are or what Shakespeare's characters go through, what Shakespeare did with them was to explore what it is to be human.

He tied the head to the heart, not just writing kings or clowns or drunken knights, but thinking, feeling humans, cutting their chests open on stage and sharing with the audience the turmoil, the passion, and the heartache that's whirling around inside them.

With Shakespeare's characters, it is always the heart that lights the fire, that sparks the brain, that makes them speak.

It leaves the characters open to endless interpretation, and keeps the plays alive and kicking.

Scene 5

Venice, Verona, Vienna

Sitting in one of Elizabethan London's many taverns, Shakespeare would have overheard stories of far-off lands while he got drunk. Chatting to sailors and travellers, hearing of Venice, and a bridge called the Rialto where all the trading was done, perhaps got him to thinking that it might be a good setting for a play.

Some think that because there's no evidence of Shakespeare travelling — yet his plays are set all over Europe — someone else must have written them. It's much more convincing, some think, that Christopher Marlowe faked his own murder, travelled around the world and sent the plays back, letting 'Shakespeare' take the credit for them.

But Shakespeare's knowledge of geography is famously inaccurate. He refers to places as being close neighbours when in fact they're nowhere near each other. He writes, not as if he's visited these distant, great cities, but as if he read about them, or had them described to him.

There's no talk of canals in *The Merchant of Venice*, but he does mention the Rialto bridge a number of times. Until I visited the city, I had no real idea of exactly how many canals there are. Of course, I knew there were canals there, but I hadn't quite appreciated the scale of the place. I saw a map of 17th-century Venice, and the only landmark amid a labyrinth of canals and buildings was the impressively grand Rialto bridge. If there's one thing you remember, you remember the Rialto.

Imagine Shakespeare, looking for inspiration to write a new play, meeting a traveller in a tavern, and the traveller says: 'So there's this beautiful city, canals and little bridges everywhere, but there's this one bridge called the Rialto, a bit like our London Bridge but not as big, where all the trading is done, and the money-lenders meet there every day ...'

He set his plays in *his* concept of Italy, France, Egypt – as well as all over Britain – in places that a great deal of his audience would probably never visit. He could show them worlds they'd never go to.

In some respects, then, painting an accurate picture wasn't as important as painting a vivid one. An average Elizabethan might not have visited Venice, or Egypt, but they might have heard of the Rialto, the pyramids and the River Nile, and have fixed ideas of what they'd be like if they did see them.

Shakespeare grew up in Warwickshire, very near the Forest of Arden, yet happily, in *As You Like It*, he has one of his characters savaged by a lion in the forest. Lions in England? He knew there weren't such things there, but

Warwickshire was a few days' horse-ride from London. Stretch the truth a little to make the story a lot more exciting ...

Shakespeare wasn't trying to write a documentary with perfect images of these places, he was writing studies of the heart and soul; and using his and his audience's ideas of them as backdrops.

They could visit these places in their mind while watching his plays. His writing and their imagination took them there. First class.

Scene 6

The mind of a 21st-century fellow

To be, or not to be – that is the question ...

All the world's a stage, and all the men and women merely players ...

A horse! A horse! My kingdom for a horse.

Even someone who claims not to know anything about Shakespeare has probably heard at least one of these quotes. They're a few of the most famous lines Shakespeare wrote. They stick with you when you hear them, and they do that for a couple of very good reasons.

They're written in a type of poetry which has the same rhythm as natural English speech (I'll deal with this particular type of poetry in detail later). A consequence of writing in this rhythm is that it's easy to remember – a particularly useful thing for busy actors with little or no rehearsal time.

They're also pretty darned cool quotes. The ideas that Shakespeare conveyed within this tight framework of poetry are *huge*. Someone once said Shakespeare wrote every thought that has ever been thunk. Thought. I don't know if that's categorically true, but all too often I've known people try to put into words a moment or a sentiment from life and then discover that Shakespeare got there first and expressed the same thought more succinctly and articulately. His writing spoke to queens and it spoke to commoners, and, staggeringly, it still speaks to us some 400 years later.

But then some things don't change. Every day, people find themselves questioning their own mortality, their place in the world in relation to everyone else, finding themselves in situations where in that moment they would give up everything they own for something they don't have. *To be, or not to be … All the world's a stage … A horse, a horse …*

Shakespeare endures. I've seen a Brazilian production of *Romeo and Juliet* that made me sob, a Slovakian production of *The Merry Wives of Windsor* that had me rolling in the aisles, and a Japanese *Pericles* that was one of the most heartbreaking pieces of theatre I've ever seen, despite knowing no Portuguese, Slovakian or Japanese.

The American actor Orson Welles once said: 'Shakespeare speaks to everyone.' His plays are set all over the world, and yet most could be set anywhere, in any country. He doesn't just write about what it is to be English, he writes about what it is to be human, and that opens his writing up to the world.

There are parts of Shakespeare that we're beginning to

lose touch with, that we have to work at: certain aspects of the language (which we'll look at in Act 3) and some of the cultural references – the context – need a little getting to grips with.

Looking at these things, and taking ourselves out of the mindset of the 21st century, will help us understand (perhaps even, dare I say it, laugh at) some of those 400-year-old jokes ...

Scene 7

Walford, home of the God of Love

Shakespeare's inventiveness (remember the 1,700 new words he coined), his ability to play with language and his poetic skill are some of the greatest innovations the English language has ever seen. But that doesn't get round the fact that many people struggle with his writing.

So here's the thing: if Shakespeare found himself practically forced to write to earn a living, and the stage, the setting – everything – helped him create such a vividly dramatic world, why did he write in what many people now think of as an 'awkward and incomprehensible' way? *O for a muse of fire* and whatnot?

Many people think they talked like that in Elizabethan England on a day-to-day basis, and to be honest, for a while I thought they did too. I was really rather surprised (and a little disappointed) to find that although the way people talk in Shakespeare's plays was *similar* to how Elizabethans spoke, it would have been rare for your average Elizabethan to speak in such a flowery way.

So if we find Shakespeare's language a bit unusual, and

the audience that went to see his plays would have found it a bit unfamiliar too, why on earth *did* he write like that?

The answer is surprisingly straightforward: by heightening his language he made it more dramatic. It's too easy to forget that his language is not of the book, but of the theatre and of the stage …

Back on the stage in the Elizabethan theatre, watching Elizabethan actors acting out situations we'd never live in, looking wonderful, speaking in this slightly unusual way – and everything so different from 'us'. Would they ever speak like us?

Well maybe, because sometimes in all the madness we need to hear something reassuringly familiar, to let us know Everything Is Okay. And, it must be remembered, this is supposed to be entertaining, a story is being told, so common speech will help everyone pick up the plot if they get lost.

But should a king speak like us? Or the God of Love? Or an Italian? Surely it wouldn't sound right. Now we're on the subject, how do you make kings, dukes and princes sound different from 'us', while using regular 17th-century London speech?

Putting on another accent wasn't an option: nowadays, if we want to make someone sound like a king, we can put on a posh accent. But people didn't start thinking of someone's accent as being indicative of their intelligence or their social status until relatively recently. The so-called 'posh' accent we know of today is only 200 years old. Not only did this accent simply not exist in Elizabethan times, the ideology of it being a thing you could use to segregate yourself from others didn't exist either.

Original pronunciation

We have a fairly good idea of what Shakespeare's accent would have sounded like. There have been two 'original pronunciation' experiments at the Globe in London, and the accent they used is thought to be about 80 per cent right.

How did they work it out? Well, if you go to see a Shakespeare play, you might notice that not all the rhymes actually rhyme when they should. This is because English pronunciation has changed since Elizabethan times, and one of the ways we can work out what the Elizabethan accent would have been like is by looking at the rhymes.

In *A Midsummer Night's Dream* (Act 3, Scene 2, lines 118–19), Puck says:

Then will two at once woo one –
That must needs be sport alone.

In modern English pronunciation, *one* and *alone* don't rhyme, so we know, because it's supposed to be a rhyming couplet, that in Shakespeare's time the pronunciation must have been different. In fact, we know that *one* would have sounded more like the modern English pronunciation of *own* (so rhyming with *alone*) – and so the couplet works.

Likewise, in the prologue of *Romeo and Juliet* (lines 9–12):

> The fearful passage of their death-marked love
> And the continuance of their parents' rage
> Which, but their children's end, naught could remove,
> Is now the two hour's traffic of our stage …

From the rhyme scheme, we can work out that *remove* would have been pronounced [ree-muv], rhyming with *love* [luv].

There are pronunciation dictionaries written at the time that can help give us an idea of how their speech sounded. Plus, the Elizabethans spelt their words more closely to how they spoke them. *Film* is spelt *philome* in *Romeo and Juliet*, so we know it was a two-syllable word, like the Irish pronunciation [fil-um].

Kings and peasants, lords and commoners all would have spoken like this, though their vocabulary and word ordering would have been quite different from each other, depending on the amount of education they'd received.

There's a popular myth that the early colonists of America, having left England around Shakespeare's time, continued to speak in Elizabethan English, but it's most definitely a myth. While language does move slower when isolated from other languages, the Pilgrim Fathers had too much contact with other peoples and accents for any real trace of Elizabethan pronunciation to have survived into modern American speech.

Using a country accent to show that someone wasn't very clever wouldn't have made sense to Shakespeare's audience. As we'll see in the next Act, in *King Lear* the character of Kent disguises himself by shaving his head and dressing as a commoner, and at one point goes *out of his dialect* (in this case, *dialect* means the type of words he uses and the way he uses them), but at no point does it say that he changes his *accent* to make himself appear more common.

So if you can't make your characters show social status by getting your actors to use different accents, how *can* you do it?

Shakespeare did it with poetry, and we'll deal with how in Act 4.

But before we get to that good stuff, some issues with the language need to be taken care of.

Act 3

Listen Carefully

Scene 1

The year 2001

Here's a line from the King James Bible (1611):

> The spirit indeed is willing, but the flesh is weak
> (Matthew 26:41)

A friend of mine works on the development of Artificial Intelligence (AI). Apparently, one of the biggest problems with successful AI is Natural Human Language Processing – in other words, getting a computer to tell the difference between, for example, the economic sense of the word *depression* and the psychological sense. A good way of testing an AI's language processing ability is to get it to translate a phrase from language A into language B, and back again. In one of my friend's experiments, the computer took the line above from the Bible, translated it into Russian, then translated it back into English. It came out with:

> The whisky is great, but the steak is terrible

It's good, but it's not great. I know next to nothing about AI, but I do know that translation is an incredibly difficult thing for a computer to do – even an artificially intelligent one. It still made me chuckle. What would it do with Hamlet's 'To be, or not to be …'? I know it would be hard (though not impossible) to translate into Chinese Mandarin – a language that doesn't have the verb 'to be' in its system.

Shall I live, or shall I kill myself? just doesn't cut it somehow. It misses the beauty of the poetry, and part of the beauty comes from the not knowing, the way the meaning slips and slides in and out of your reach.

KLINGON CHANCELLOR GORKON: You have not experienced Shakespeare until you have read him in the original Klingon.

KLINGON: Tak Pah, Tak Beh …

ALL: (laughter)

from the 1991 film *Star Trek VI: The Undiscovered Country*

That's the problem with translation and adaptations. They try to make something easier to digest, but can end up taking the heart out of it. When it comes to Shakespeare, faced with the peculiar-looking poetry and the 400-year-old words, many people will turn to translated copies of the plays; indeed, adapting or translating Shakespeare into 'modern' English has become a bit of a fad in recent times.

There's a growing number of people who feel that you can get rid of the Olde language, make it all fresh and modern, and it'll stay the same.

It won't, of course. Part of the problem with Shakespeare's plays is, as we saw earlier, that the stories aren't original. Nor are they flawless. Translate, update, adapt Shakespeare's writing, and all you're really left with is the story. Take the poetry away, and you very quickly realise you're pulling at a piece of string that will make everything unravel.

Shakespeare didn't seem to care so much about the actual stories he was telling as much as he did about the characters and the language he used to tell them. There are plot holes in *Hamlet* you can drive buses through. Shakespeare *is* the poetry and the language, pulled together by the man's wit and his take on old stories, and all of it driving towards one end: creating some truly terrific drama.

More to the point, a lot of Shakespeare's writing doesn't actually need translating. The English language the Elizabethans spoke is known as Early Modern English (as opposed to the English spoken 200 years before – Middle English, which was the English of Chaucer). Just from a vocabulary point of view, Early Modern English isn't really that different from Modern English, the language I'm using now; as I said in Act 1, only 5 per cent of all the words Shakespeare used are difficult enough to need a definition.

There are parts of Shakespeare that *do* need work to understand them, but by completely rewriting the poetry, the beauty of what is being said is often lost. And Shakespeare without the poetry is The Beatles' 'Long and Winding Road' covered by Cher. Sure, you *could* listen to it, I suppose, but the heart of the song lies with Paul's delivery.

Most modern adaptations and translations don't encourage us to learn how to understand the original texts. There are some that do. A new series of graphic novels published in November 2007 provides three versions of the same play: an original text, a plain (modern) text, and a 'quick' text. I'm not sure about the other two, but at least they've used the original text as well as the updated versions.

I have a *Manga* graphic novel adaptation of *Hamlet* which also uses the original text. Like the Baz Luhrmann film of *Romeo + Juliet*, the play is heavily edited down, but the fact that they're using the original text at all, rather than updating it, is fabulous. The original words next to the crisp *Manga* drawings, just like the freshness of Luhrmann's Mexican settings, makes the play sing.

But go to an edition of Shakespeare that does away with the original text and has been translated into Modern English, and you lose the impact of Shakespeare's choice of language. But what does *that* mean exactly?

Language is made up of choices – choices of grammar,

of words, and of sound patterns. All of these things can come together with great effect, and Shakespeare was one of the first writers not only to realise this, but to openly acknowledge it. How do we know? He tells us through one of his characters.

Look at this extract, from *King Lear*. Kent is King Lear's faithful servant who's been banished from Lear's service but returns disguised as a commoner, under the name of Caius, and convinces Lear to employ him again.

He is accused by Cornwall (Lear's son-in-law, and one of the rulers of the land) of not being able to flatter, so Kent speaks as poetically as he can. Cornwall asks him why he's suddenly started to speak so differently. Kent switches back to his 'low' speech, and replies that he changed his dialect because it seemed Cornwall didn't like it:

KENT
Sir, 'tis my occupation to be plain.
I have seen better faces in my time
Than stands on any shoulder that I see
Before me at this instant.

CORNWALL   This is some fellow
Who, having been praised for bluntness, doth affect
A saucy roughness, and constrains the garb
Quite from his nature. He cannot flatter, he!
An honest mind and plain – he must speak truth!

And they will take it, so; if not, he's plain.
These kind of knaves I know, which in this plainness
Harbour more craft and more corrupter ends
Than twenty silly-ducking observants
That stretch their duties nicely.

KENT
Sir, in good faith, in sincere verity,
Under th'allowance of your great aspect
Whose influence like the wreath of radiant fire
On flickering Phoebus' front—

CORNWALL   What mean'st by this?

KENT To go out of my dialect which you discommend so
much. I know, sir, I am no flatterer.

> (Act 2, Scene 2, lines 90–108)

Kent's use of high vocabulary, complicated words and sentence structure, and the classical allusion to Phoebus (the god of the sun) which Cornwall interrupts, is a risky thing for him to do: it could betray the fact that he's in disguise, and isn't really a commoner at all. Kent is punished for the clever way he uses his language – it seems to surprise and embarrass Cornwall, who wouldn't expect a commoner to speak so articulately – but he proves his point well.

All this would be lost, in translation.

As for this idea of difficult Olde words ...

Am I a coward ...?

Boy, but Shakespeare knew how to insult someone. These days, we don't seem to be nearly so creative with our insults as the Elizabethans were, for the most part sadly limiting our exchanges to a repetitive series of swear words. Shakespeare did it so much better, from the picturesque *cockscomb* (the crest on the top of a cock's head = *fool, halfwit*) to the very commonly used *whoreson* (son of a whore = *bastard*), to this incredibly colourful outburst from Falstaff in *Henry IV Part 1*:

> You starveling, you eel-skin, you dried neat's-tongue, you bull's pizzle, you stock-fish.

> (neat = *ox*, stock-fish = *dried cod*, pizzle = I'll leave to your imaginations)

Calling someone *base* (= dishonourable) would usually upset them a fair bit, but in *King Lear*, Kent really lets rip when he calls Oswald a *base football player*. Not a particularly great insult nowadays, but football in Elizabethan times was a real game of the gutter, described by a writer of the time as a game of 'beastly fury and extreme violence' (so not that much has changed) and to be 'utterly abjected by all noblemen'. If you played football, there really wasn't any lower you could sink. Kent outdoes himself, though, a little later in the play (Act 2, Scene 2, lines 13–22), and really lets rip at Oswald, with a tremendous diatribe:

KENT: Fellow, I know thee.
OSWALD: What dost thou know me for?

Act 3, Scene 1

KENT: A knave, a rascal, an eater of broken meats, a base, proud, shallow, beggarly, three-suited, hundred-pound, filthy-worsted-stocking knave; a lily-livered, action-taking, whoreson glass-gazing super-serviceable finical rogue; one-trunk-inheriting slave; one that wouldst be a bawd in way of good service, and art nothing but the composition of a knave, beggar, coward, pander, and the son and heir of a mongrel bitch; one whom I will beat into clamorous whining if thou deniest the least syllable of thy addition.

Son and heir of a mongrel bitch ... Classy.

Scene 2

A library

The Ghost of Olde Englishe rears its ugly head. I know a lot of people think the hardest thing about Shakespeare is the difficult words.

Rather wonderfully, I can tell you it's not a big problem. I know (because I've counted them) that only a very small number of the words found in Shakespeare's works are difficult to understand.

Of the 900,000-odd words in Shakespeare, as we've seen, only 5 per cent of them would give someone wandering around the 21st century a hard time. What's more, you could go through life never understanding what they mean, this 5 per cent, and still love every one of Shakespeare's works.

Well hang on, you might say, *5 per cent is still an awful lot of words*. But that total includes words used dozens of times, like *bootless* (= useless). There are long stretches of text where we don't encounter any difficult words at all, or one of the easier ones, like *morn*.

If you look at the vocab as you would a foreign language – spend a little time learning, to stretch the analogy, how to ask for a drink in Shakespearian – then another level of his plays will open up to you.

The language he uses is something we need to take care of. We can't ignore the fact that Shakespeare is over 400 years older than us, after all, and he used different slang words, different swear words, had different ways of saying *I love you*. Not only that, but he went through a completely different education system from us, read different books as an adult, and so made different cultural references in his plays.

He would have studied Greek and been fluent in Latin (he would have had to speak Latin at school every day). If you studied a foreign language like French, German or Spanish at school you probably had about 1,500 hours of study. Shakespeare would have had over *20,000* hours of Greek and Latin study, which is at least part of the reason why there are so many references to Greek gods and bits of Latin scattered throughout his plays. That was a fairly common education in those times, so a lot of his audience would have understood these references without having to think too hard about them.

The words I used that were cool when I was younger are so out of date now. No one says 'cool' any more. Actually, I don't think anyone says '*so* out of date', or *so* anything any more, either. Whatever. No one says 'whatever' any more, and I'm sure that word was still being used last year. How, though, would you explain the *meaning* of 'whatever' to someone in ten years' time? In 100 years' time? How about in 400 years' time ...? *And* you'd have to use *their* language and their cultural references. You couldn't. At least not without a couple of books, a flip-chart, and maybe some diagrams.

It's the same with Shakespeare. We have to work to understand the way he swears, the way he makes promises, the way he uses our language (and it is, essentially, still *our* language). There's a good example about halfway through Hamlet's 'To be, or not to be' speech:

> For who would bear the Whips and Scornes of time ...
> When he himself might his *Quietus* make
> With a bare Bodkin?
>
> (*Hamlet*, Act 3, Scene 1, lines 70–6)

There are probably two words there that you'd miss the meaning of, if you were just reading it by yourself. There's a good chance you'd understand it fine if you saw it being acted. But even then, seeing it acted, knowing that *Quietus* means *release* and a *Bodkin* is a *dagger* helps enormously (in this instance, a *bare* bodkin means an unadorned, plain dagger). Who would live through the harshness of life, he says, when you could end it all with a simple tool like a dagger?

I have a confession to make. I just looked those words up. I used to know what they meant, but I'd forgotten. No one knows what *all* the words in Shakespeare mean, and everyone needs to look words up – especially words like *bare* that are still in our vocabulary today but which had a variety of different meanings 400 years ago.

Exactly because of that need, I co-wrote a dictionary of all of Shakespeare's difficult words a couple of years ago. It's quite a hefty tome, as we made sure every word we defined included as many of the different meanings we could think of that Shakespeare might have meant – and I particularly made sure we thought of nuances from a theatrical point of view. In Shakespeare's time, *bare* also meant *unsheathed*. It also meant *wretched*. Which sense of the word Hamlet means is up to the actor and the director working on the production, or you, the reader.

Of course, when you're watching Shakespeare being acted, a lot of these problems won't be a factor. The meaning of a difficult word gets buoyed up by the rest of the sentence when spoken out loud, and acting Shakespeare always helps define meaning much more than silent reading ever could.

Many of the words you'll find in a Shakespeare play might look similar or be identical to words you use every day. If it looks even slightly like a word you know, the chances are it'll mean what you think it means.

However. There are some words, known as *false friends*, that will mislead you. *Doubt*, in Shakespeare's time, meant *fear*. When Regan, in *King Lear*, says to Edmund, 'Our sister's man is certainly miscarried' (my sister's servant has definitely failed), Edmund's response is: ''Tis to be doubted, madam.' But he isn't questioning her, he's agreeing with her. 'It is something to be feared', he's saying.

All this can take a little getting used to, but considering that (linguistically speaking) we're travelling hundreds of years back in time, we could be worse off than 5 per cent.

Here are twenty false friends you might come across …

False friend	Modern meaning(s)	Obsolete meaning(s)
adventure (noun)	dangerous, risky or exciting undertaking	venture, enterprise; experience
bootless (adverb)	without boots	uselessly, unsuccessfully
distracted (adjective)	unfocused, anxious	confused, near madness; divided, torn apart
doubt (verb)	hesitate to believe	fear, be afraid
excrement (noun)	waste matter discharged from the bowels	outgrowth (of hair, nails, or feathers)
fabulous (adjective)	marvellous; astonishing	mythical, invented

False friend	Modern meaning(s)	Obsolete meaning(s)
habit (noun)	usual manner of behaviour	costume, clothing
lover (noun)	partner in a sexual relationship	companion, dear friend
mean (adjective)	spiteful, nasty; not generous	of low rank; lowly, humble; unworthy
mercly (adverb)	only (and nothing more)	utterly, entirely
naughty (adjective)	badly behaved; improper	wicked, evil
nice (adjective)	agreeable, pleasant	lustful; foolish; fastidious; uncertain; trivial; minutely detailed; subtle; skilful
quick (adjective)	rapid, swift	alive, full of life; lively, animated
revolve (verb)	perform a circular motion	consider, ponder, meditate
sad (adjective)	expressing grief or unhappiness	serious, grave, solemn

False friend	Modern meaning(s)	Obsolete meaning(s)
safe (adjective)	unharmed, secure	sure, certain; safely out of the way; harmless, not dangerous
sensible (adjective)	endowed with good sense	capable of receiving sensation; responsive; evident
silly (adjective)	foolish, stupid	helpless; lowly; simple
table (noun)	piece of furniture	notebook
want (verb)	desire, wish, need	lack, be without

13th-century England. A field

Ask someone to 'speak Shakespearian' and they'll probably throw in a couple of phrases like *thou art a blaggard* or *thou art an arse*, without knowing why they're saying *thou* instead of *you*. An awful lot of people coming to Shakespeare don't know why both these second-person pronouns (to give them their official title) are there, and often want to change all the *thous* to *yous* to make everything look neat and tidy.

Why can't we – or shouldn't we – ignore them?

Ever learnt French? If you have, you'll know that there are two ways of saying *you*. A polite and formal way (*vous*), which can be used to address one person or a group of people; and a more sociable and informal way (*tu*), which is used only when speaking to one person.

There used to be a similar option in the English language: in Old English, *thou* was used to address one person and *you* was used to address more than one. But from the 13th century onwards, in Middle English, *you* started to develop an added connotation of politeness, probably because people wanted to copy the respected French way of speaking; and they began to use *you* in one-on-one conversations. The assumption was that if you spoke French, you must therefore be rich and intelligent; and those who couldn't afford to learn French simply changed their own language to sound more learned.

So by the time Shakespeare was writing – when our language was known as Early Modern English – there was a choice:

Opener	Used when	Normal reply
you	upper classes are talking to each other, even when they're closely related	you
thou	lower classes are talking to each other	thou
thou	superiors are talking to inferiors, for instance:	
	§ parents to children	you
	§ masters to servants	you
thou	for special intimacy, for instance:	
	§ talking to a lover	thou
	§ addressing God or a god (e.g. Jupiter)	you
thou	a character talks to someone absent	—
thou	a character talks to someone near to them on stage	thou
you	a character talks to someone far away from them on stage	you

When going through a play, you'll find *thou* and *you* in various different forms, depending on how they're being used:

> The *thou*-forms are *thou, thee, thy, thine,* and *thyself.*
> *You*-forms are *you, your, yours,* and *yourself/yourselves.*

In a scene, when someone changes from using *thou* to using *you*, or the other way round, *it always means something* – Shakespeare consciously chose when to switch between them – and it usually implies a change of attitude, or a new emotion or mood.

It could be anything: a sign of extra affection or of anger; an insult or a compliment; a piece of playfulness or an indication that the speaker is adopting a more business-like or professional attitude, distancing themselves socially or physically; or trying to become more formal or informal.

A modern-day equivalent might be how you choose to address your boss, when you're already on first-name terms. If I walk into work and say *Hi John* to my boss and he replies *Hello Mr Crystal*, I sure as hell will address him more formally next time we encounter each other. I'd have to be either very confident in myself or very foolhardy to keep calling him *John* once he's established that formality between us. Likewise, if the next day my boss calls me *Ben*, then I've got a pretty good chance of calling him by his first name again, and it wouldn't be considered too informal.

That said, if the Queen were to call me *Ben* I'm fairly sure she wouldn't be very happy if I called her *Liz*. The rules of formality and social hierarchy that we follow today apply in a very similar way to how *thou* and *you* is used in Shakespeare.

As well as the sociological aspect, the intimacy that is implied when saying *thou* to someone is a good indicator to an actor to be physically close to the person they're talking to on stage.

A good starting point when acting or reading Shakespeare for the first time is to always be aware of whether the characters are using *thou* or *you* to each other.

If they're using *thou* to each other, and there are other people not involved in the dialogue, can those other people hear what's being said? If they've been using *thou* to each other, but then one character switches to *you*, what made that character switch? Do they feel insulted? What might have made their attitude change?

There are hundreds of examples of this happening scattered throughout the plays, and either as an actor, a reader, or simply a watcher of Shakespeare, not to be aware of the changes is to ignore a great part of his intention when he was writing.

A couple, like Beatrice and Benedick in *Much Ado About Nothing*, starting to use *thou* to each other when they haven't before, is a little like when you start a relationship with someone nowadays, and begin to call them *honey* or *darling*, *sweetheart* or *love*.

Conversely, when two characters stop using it to each other, it equally means a great deal. Using this writing technique, something of great import can be subtly conveyed without anything more direct being said out loud.

There's a great and often-missed moment right at the beginning of *Hamlet* – considering it's the opening ten lines, Shakespeare packs an awful lot of back-story into very few words. Looking at the second-person pronouns and their variant forms, you can gather a lot of information about what's happening (the italics aren't there to show stress, only to point out pronouns):

BARNARDO: Who's there?

FRANCISCO: Nay, answer me. Stand and unfold *yourself*.

BARNARDO: Long live the King!

FRANCISCO: Barnardo?

BARNARDO: He.

FRANCISCO: *You* come most carefully upon *your* hour.

BARNARDO: 'Tis now struck twelve. Get *thee* to bed, Francisco.

FRANCISCO: For this relief much thanks. 'Tis bitter cold, And I am sick at heart.

BARNARDO: Have *you* had quiet guard?

Two men encounter each other. Francisco, a guard on duty hearing someone call to him, assumes his authority and demands the other man show himself, and he uses the formal *yourself* to do it. Because both men have asked the other for identification, and particularly as Francisco is being formal, we can assume that either it's too dark or Barnardo is too far away for Francisco to see clearly, or both.

Barnardo gives the password, an affirmation of Friend rather than Foe, with 'Long live the King' – a formal greeting that would imply they're at a more heightened state of watch than normal.

Once identity is established, Francisco responds formally, courteously, with *you*, one professional talking to another: '*You* come most carefully upon *your* hour.'

By the time they seem to physically meet, Barnardo becomes more informal and chatty: he uses '*Tis* instead of 'it is', and he switches to the more friendly *thee* when he sends Francisco off to bed:

BARNARDO: 'Tis now struck twelve. Get *thee* to bed,
  Francisco.
FRANCISCO: For this relief much thanks. 'Tis bitter cold,
  And I am sick at heart.

So we find out it's twelve o'clock, and cold, Francisco's being sent off to bed, so it *is* most likely night-time; Barnardo is the relieving guard, and we find out a little later that they've been on guard like this for a few days now … But why?

> FRANCISCO: For this relief much thanks. 'Tis bitter cold,
>   And I am sick at heart.

Thank goodness for that, says Francisco, *it's bloody cold and I'm not happy about any of this.*

For some reason, in response to what Francisco has just said, Barnardo immediately switches from using the *thou* form of 'Get *thee* to bed' back to the *you* form:

> BARNARDO: Have *you* had quiet guard?

Now why would he do that? There must be more to 'I am sick at heart' than *I'm ill* or *I'm tired*, to provoke a change of formality from Barnardo.

As we later find out, they're on guard because a ghost has been seen walking the battlements, so they must be pretty on edge (thus the formal 'Friend or Foe' opening). Perhaps Barnardo thinks Francisco saw the ghost while he was on duty. 'Have *you* had quiet guard?', asks Barnardo, switching to the *you* of professional soldier and boss that he used when he entered, rather than the *thee* of a friend and colleague that came a little later.

To the relief of both, Francisco gives a curious, and

probably pointed but welcome reply: 'Not a Mouse stir-ring …'

An incredible amount of subtext and back-story, all glaringly obvious once you know what you're looking for, and most of it simply conveyed with a couple of pronouns.

There are some great *thou/you* instances in Shakes-peare, which can lead to intense discussions in a rehearsal room.

In *Othello*, both Desdemona and Othello always use *thou* to Iago, and *you* to Cassio. Is that a sign of great respect and intimacy to Iago, or is it a great affront, seeing that the *you* form is technically more formal (and so more respect-ful)?

It's hard to say, but saying *thou* to someone could some-times be taken as an insult – in *Twelfth Night*, Sir Toby Belch advises Andrew Aguecheek to insult his enemy by calling him *thou*.

Particularly interesting for us, in anticipation of the final Act of this book, is what Shakespeare does in *Macbeth*.

The relationship between Macbeth and his wife is one of many fascinating relationships that Shakespeare scripted, and the complexity of the relationship is reflected in the way they refer to each other.

To begin with, the forms they use suggest a great close-ness (take a look at Act 1, Scene 5 – the letter scene – to see her changing use of *thou* and *you*), but very quickly we find a relationship that shifts in respect, formality, and intimacy. After Act 1, Scene 7 – once Macbeth has tried to convince his wife that they shouldn't kill Duncan – Lady Macbeth never uses *thou* to her husband again.

It's a subtle change in the use of pronouns that would seem to imply she's lost a certain degree of love and respect for her husband ...

All of these things – the pronouns, the need for the original phrasing and the particular words he chose to use – are ingredients to the big birthday cake that is the poetry Shakespeare wrote. But before I cut a big slice for you, there's a main course to take care of ...

Scene 4

A Christmas tree, Liverpool

When I started writing this book, I found a report in a newspaper that described new research by a scientist in Liverpool. The scientist said that when you read Shakespeare, the extra work that the poetry and the unfamiliar words require makes a part of the temporal lobe of your brain known as the *Sylvian Fissure* light up like a Christmas tree.

Basically, he said, reading Shakespeare, and taking the time to work through the hard words and the poetry, makes you smarter.

I'm not going to pretend that everyone loves poetry. Personally speaking, I used to despise it.

But a Shakespeare director, a very nice bearded chap called Patrick Tucker, told me once that Shakespeare's poetry has a system to it; that it's full of hidden clues from Shakespeare telling his actors how to deliver his lines; and that once you know how, the poetry is practically colour-coded, virtually letting you read it by numbers. Alan Turing and Dan Brown eat your heart out.

Before I'd learnt this system in Shakespeare, it seemed like poetry was surrounded by a vast amount of technical terminology used by very flouncy people, and so either required too much work that I didn't want to do, or a goatee and a hat, neither of which I had. I had an overall sense that I just really didn't get it, that poetry was a club I wanted to join but which didn't want me as a member.

It felt a bit like when I wanted to get into jazz, but knew nothing about the music: I knew only that there were hundreds of artists waiting to be discovered, that it was generally thought of as being inaccessible unless you understood it (which just seemed ridiculous), and I had been told by others that it was a chaotic, disorganised sort of music ... I had no idea where and how to begin, really only knowing that if I did find a way in, I'd probably be hooked forever.

Thank you, Miles Davis. When I listened to his record *Kind of Blue*, it seemed so simple to begin with. The repetitive themes sounded basic, and the other instruments seemed disjointed, completely separate from each other. But Davis was a genius too, and listening again, I realised the themes were actually quite beautifully complicated, the instruments were in a sort of a-rhythmic harmony. My ears just weren't used to what was going on. The way Davis played jazz, he led you into his world, and taught you how to listen to his music. Shakespeare did the same for me with poetry.

With poetry, though, I had already been struggling for

some time to understand it technically, having learnt a rather stringent set of rules on How To Take A Poem Apart … though the word *deconstruct* was more than likely used instead. And this is part of the problem when looking at poetry: a lot of fancy names are given to what are essentially very simple ideas.

One simple idea, in particular, causes a lot of trouble. Specifically, a type of poetry that was incredibly popular while Shakespeare was an up-and-coming writer, looking for a nice cash bunny to set him up.

So popular was this particular type of poetry, and so varied were the ways of using it, that he dedicated most of his writing career to mastering, playing with, and perfecting the style. Indeed, 'it' remained the popular style of poetry for the rest of his life, and for quite a time beyond, partly due to his own success in writing it. What is this particular, popular, money-spinning style of writing poetry called?

You've probably heard its name.

Take a deep breath, and say it with me. Whisper it …

… iambic pentameter …

Good. I'm glad we got through that together, so now let's deal with it. Like a sticking plaster, let's get it over and done with, and rip it off quick.

Why do we have to deal with it in the first place? Why

can't we get away with ignoring it and pretending it isn't there? Because to do so would be to ignore the bulk of what Shakespeare is. Shakespeare saw potential in iambic pentameter, in a similar way to the programmers who saw the basic search engines, and invented Google.

Understand iambic pentameter and you understand Shakespeare.

For whatever reason – although I imagine the phrase itself is part of the problem – iambic pentameter is the main stumbling block with Shakespeare, where most people, myself included, have fallen. Those words confused me more than I'd like or care to admit.

They seemed like a very pointless pairing of difficult academic words, used to describe even more pointless, difficult words. Of course, they're nothing of the sort, but that's the way I felt at the time. So many of the good things about Shakespeare seemed shrouded in mystery and out of my reach, hidden behind other, similarly impenetrable words.

Nowadays when I run workshops and say those dreaded words, a shiver runs through everyone like I've set a curse. A dark cloud falls over the room. A look of fear enters everyone's eyes …

But what 'it' is, is simple. What it means is a little more complicated, but you could go through the rest of your life thoroughly enjoying Shakespeare on a rudimentary level and know only that iambic pentameter was the popular style of writing poetry in Shakespeare's time.

Think about it in terms of Italian opera. I don't speak Italian, but I could go to an opera sung in Italian and I'd enjoy it on a basic level: I'd revel in the fights, the lights, the sounds, and the raw emotions. Or I could (and one day, I promise myself, I will) learn a little Italian, maybe read the libretto before I go.

Or, in this case, learn a bit of Shakespearian before going to see a play of his, and unlock a treasure chest of life-changing jewels in his work.

I'm getting a little carried away. Everything we've looked at so far are the doors and windows to the House of Shakespeare.

The foundation of it all, though, is poetry. Understand how iambic pentameter works, and you can talk to Shakespeare.

I mean it. You can have a conversation with him.

Act 4

Catch the Rhythm

Scene 1

Theatre Way, Wigan

Before we dig into iambic pentameter itself, an important distinction needs to be made. There are two main types of speech in Shakespeare's plays, and they're most commonly referred to as *poetry* and *prose*.

You speak prose. *Prose* is just a word for normal, free-flowing speech or text, and although there are rules that govern it, they are neither as obvious nor as formal as the rules that you find in poetry.

It's important to note that any one word of the English language can be found in either poetry or prose – one writing style doesn't exclude a particular set of words. To be entirely accurate, perhaps I should say there are some words that are *more likely* to turn up in one style than another, but that doesn't really concern us here.

To pick a fictional character purely at random, here's the Reverend Clement Hedges, from the film *Wallace & Gromit: The Curse of the Were-Rabbit* (2005), speaking in prose:

HEDGES This was no man. Does a man have teeth the size of axe blades? Or ears like terrible tombstones? By tampering with nature, forcing vegetables to swell far beyond their natural size, we have brought a terrible judgement on ourselves.

And the same speech rewritten as poetry:

HEDGES
This was no man. Does a man have teeth
The size of axe blades? Or ears like terrible tombstones?
By tampering with nature, forcing vegetables to swell
Far beyond their natural size, we have brought
A terrible judgement on ourselves.

The words are all the same, I simply broke the speech up into lines, and that's the first giveaway with poetry. It's written in lines and at the beginning of each line the first letter is capitalised (I should say that this may not be true for some modern poetry you might come across, but in Shakespeare, this is how it is).

Now it's probably fair to say that this now-slightly-poetic extract might not be remembered in hundreds of years' time, but the techniques I used to make it pretty are the same ones that modern poets use, and they're similar to the ones Shakespeare used.

Ending lines with *Does a man have teeth* and *we have brought* makes the reader question what's going to come next. It brings an anticipation to the line, if only for a second.

It makes it more dramatic. Leaving the punchline by itself on the last line gives a comic pacing to the reading of it.

Breaking some of the standard rules of English grammar (that a new line = a new sentence, for example) to emphasise particular points of a piece of writing, as I've done with Hedges' most learned observation, is essentially what Shakespeare did.

However, what's particularly important when having a gander at Shakespeare, is how the thoughts of a character sometimes go with the lines of poetry, and sometimes the thoughts break over the lines of poetry.

A full stop usually indicates the end of a *thought*, traditionally known as a sentence, but the word *sentence* takes us back down the Literature road: they're actors' texts, so we're going to stay on Theatre Way and call them *thoughts*. People write in *sentences*, they speak in *thoughts*. If I had broken Hedges' speech up into parcels of sense, or thought, it would have looked more like this:

HEDGES
This was no man.
Does a man have teeth the size of axe blades?
Or ears like terrible tombstones?
By tampering with nature,
Forcing vegetables to swell far beyond their natural size,
We have brought a terrible judgement on ourselves.

The first thought takes up a full line of poetry. So do the second and third thoughts. But the fourth thought over-flows into three lines of poetry. The way it overflows brings a slightly different dimension to the dramatic tension of the writing.

If the poem were read out loud, the reader would need to make it clear that while the last three lines are three different lines of poetry, they are still one thought. Otherwise, when read aloud, it'll just sound like prose, and the vast effort the writer has put into writing it as poetry would be wasted.

So it's become normal practice for the end of a line of poetry to be acknowledged in the voice, somehow – a rising inflection, or a slight pause, perhaps – to indicate that while the line of poetry has ended, the thought has not.

Scene 2

A kitchen, baking verse-cake

Poetry then, as far as we're concerned, is any text that has been written in lines. *Verse* is poetry that has been given a particular rhythm. You might hear the two terms used interchangeably. I'll do my very best not to do that.

Much of Shakespeare's work is written in verse: he made his actors (and so therefore his characters too) speak a lot of the time in rhythmical poetry; a brilliantly simple device to make his kings sound kingly. This gives birth to a general rule: ordinary people speak in prose, kings and queens speak in verse (though it's not always this way round: remember earlier in the book where Kent in *King Lear*, disguised as an ordinary commoner, mocks Cornwall – he doesn't just use complicated words to go 'out of his dialect', he switches into verse, the speech of kings, and back again to prose. We'll see more of this later.).

The hierarchy of speech in Shakespeare, going from a low emotional intensity and a prosaic language, to high emotion and very poetic language, goes like this:

Song

↑

Sonnet

↑

Rhyming verse

↑

Blank verse
(verse that doesn't rhyme)

↑

Prose

If you're trying to express something that prose won't do justice to, then switch to blank verse. If that isn't forceful enough, moving up to rhyming verse or a sonnet (a fourteen-line rhyming poem) might do it: when Romeo and Juliet first meet and dance together, Shakespeare gives them a sonnet to share, to convey to the audience the height of their emotions and the importance of their first meeting (I'll look at sonnets in a bit more detail later on in this Act).

But if your emotions can't be expressed in any other way, then you just gotta sing! Desdemona's willow song in Act 4, Scene 3 of *Othello*, and Ophelia's terribly sad song in Act 4, Scene 5 of *Hamlet* are beautiful examples.

Verse is why a lot of people think Shakespeare writes in an odd-looking way – why the plays look so different from modern English when you see them on the page – and is probably a large part of the reason why many people take one look and say *Shakespeare wrote in a different language.*

Here are a couple of examples from Shakespeare, first verse from *Hamlet*, then prose from *Much Ado About Nothing*:

HAMLET
To be, or not to be – that is the question;
Whether 'tis nobler in the mind to suffer
The slings and arrows of outrageous fortune
Or to take arms against a sea of troubles
And by opposing end them.

(Act 3, Scene 1, lines 56–60)

BENEDICK (coming forward) This can be no trick. The conference was sadly borne. They have the truth of this from Hero. They seem to pity the lady; it seems her affections have their full bent. Love me?

(Act 2, Scene 3, lines 215–18)

Sometimes Shakespeare writes in verse, sometimes he writes in prose. As we saw earlier (pp. 88–9) with the Kent/ Cornwall extract from *King Lear*, sometimes he switches from one to the other in the same scene, in the same conversation between two characters, and like a lot of the other innocuous-looking inconsistencies in Shakespeare's writing, this can either be ignored, or be seen as a good character note.

With the *King Lear* example, in order to emphasise Kent's switch from high, flowery language back to his commoner's tongue, Shakespeare makes him switch back to prose. Using Caius' voice again, and taking away the beauty of verse, Kent's reply is twice as powerful.

Shakespeare could have written Benedick's speech in verse, and it might have looked something like this:

BENEDICK
This can be no trick. The conference was sadly borne.
They have the truth of this from Hero. They seem
To pity the lady; it seems her affections
Have their full bent. Love me?

But Shakespeare *didn't* write it in verse. For some reason, for this moment in Benedick's life, Shakespeare wanted him to speak in prose. Benedick speaks in verse elsewhere in the play, so why not here? Well, there are probably a dozen reasons. Verse would force the actor to deliver the lines more dramatically, and perhaps, as Benedick is alone on stage, he's more relaxed and so he doesn't feel the need to heighten the style of his speech.

Whatever the reason, the point is that there *is always a reason* why one character speaks in prose, another in verse, or the same character switches styles during a scene. (As we'll see later, modern editors of Shakespeare sometimes change lines which are prose in the Folio to verse.) It's one of a number of clues that Shakespeare left in his writing for his actors to find, so that they'd speak his words in the exact way he wanted them to, without his ever having to ask them directly.

Verse or prose?

Carrying on the idea that Shakespeare used verse to make his kings sound kingly, it's not surprising that the only plays he wrote entirely in verse are about kings:

King Edward III
King John
Richard II

Both sequels to *King Henry VI* are almost entirely written in verse, and *Titus Andronicus*, *Richard III* and *Henry VIII* also come close to being prose-less.

At the other end of the spectrum, none of his surviving plays is written entirely in prose.

The Merry Wives of Windsor has the greatest amount of prose, at 87 per cent, with *Much Ado About Nothing* and *Twelfth Night* next in line – but even 38 per cent of *Twelfth Night* is verse.

Verse seemed to bake Shakespeare's (and, it would seem, his audience's) cake more than prose ...

Scene 3

A cardiac unit

Unless it's written down, it can be quite hard for us to tell the difference between verse and prose, and an Elizabethan audience might not have been able to notice the difference either, for a couple of very good reasons.

One, as I said earlier, they'd probably never have read the texts beforehand, so they wouldn't be able to see that what they were listening to was written in poetry – and as I've just shown, it's very easy to spot when written down.

And two, the beauty of iambic pentameter is that it's the style of poetry that most closely resembles English speech.

I think that's brilliant. At a time when the English language (as we know it today) was relatively new and exciting, the most popular style of poetry imitated its natural rhythm when spoken out loud. What's even more exciting is that Shakespeare used this very human-sounding poetry to explore what it is to be human.

Shakespeare's audience watched actors pretending to be people they weren't, in situations that they'd probably never get to experience, wearing unusual clothes, often saying quite extraordinary things, *but even when they were pretending to be kings, still sounding like you and me.*

SHAKESPEARE ON TOAST

I said earlier that verse is a type of poetry that has a particular rhythm. Your heartbeat has a particular rhythm, too – a (hopefully!) regular *weak-strong, weak-strong* pulse. The natural rhythm of the English language is very similar to that – an alternating contrast between strong-sounding syllables and weak-sounding syllables. It should come as no surprise, then, that a lot of poetry written in English has this heartbeat-like rhythm to it. Prose also reflects the rhythm of everyday English speech but, unlike poetry, it doesn't have regular rhythmical units, and there aren't structured rules for the number of syllables per line, as we're about to see.

Rhythm in poetry is known as *metre*; poetry with a steady, regular rhythm is known as *metrical poetry*. Here's a classic example of such a thing:

Shall I compare thee to a summer's day?
(Sonnet 18, opening line)

When asking questions about a piece of metrical poetry, there are two things you need to find out:

— What *kind* of rhythm does it have?
— *How many* beats are there?

Now. The phrase *iambic pentameter* is a fancy way of answering these questions, and is actually saying a very simple thing: it's telling you, in a complicated way, the kind of rhythm, and how many beats (or units of rhythm) there should be in the line.

The word *meter* in *pentameter* is the same word as *metre*, and it has the same meaning – it's talking about a rhythmical line of poetry – but it unhelpfully has a different spelling.

The other half of the word – *penta* – is Greek and means *five*, so we know that in this rhythmical line of poetry there will be five things.

When people look at lines of poetry written in metre, they count in units of rhythm. A unit of rhythm is known as a *foot* – so they count in *metrical feet*. Usually, a pair of syllables makes up one metrical foot. It follows then that a line of verse that has ten syllables in it, as ours does, has *five feet* (which, as my mother would say, makes it difficult to buy shoes for):

syllables	1st	2nd	3rd	4th	5th	6th	7th	8th	9th	10th
feet		1		2		3		4		5

Shall - I - com-pare-thee - to - a - sum-mer's-day?

A line of poetry with ten rhythmically ordered syllables (five metrical feet) is a line of *pentameter*. A line of poetry with four metrical feet is called *tetrameter*, three metrical feet *trimeter*, and so on.

Back to the two questions – we know how many beats there are (five), so what kind of rhythm is it?

We hear a rhythm when we hear a recurring pattern of strong and weak beats, so really we're asking which are the strongly stressed syllables and which the weak?

There are several possibilities in metrical poetry, but here are the two main types of metrical feet (I've used **BOLD CAPITALS** to make it as clear as possible where the stronger stress is):

§ An *iambic* foot. In Greek, an *iamb* means a weak syllable followed by a strong (*de-DUM*). A naturally iambic word is *com-PARE*.

§ A *trochaic* foot. The opposite of an iamb, a *trochee* (pronounced *TROH-key*) means the syllables go strong-weak (*DUM-de*). A naturally trochaic word is *E-asy*. So is *TRO-chee*, for that matter.

If an iambic foot sounds like *de-DUM*, then five iambs together would look like this:

syllables 1st 2nd 3rd 4th 5th 6th 7th 8th 9th 10th
sound de-**DUM** de-**DUM** de-**DUM** de-**DUM** de-**DUM**

Say it out loud. One *de-DUM* every second, patting your

hand on your leg every *DUM*. It doesn't really matter how fast you say it, as long as the rhythm is constant:

de-**DUM** de-**DUM** de-**DUM** de-**DUM** de-**DUM**

That is a line of iambic pentameter – a line of metre with five iambic feet.

Ten syllables evenly stressed *weak-STRONG*, or stressed *iambically*, means that the weak stresses should always be on the odd syllables – the 1st, 3rd, 5th, 7th and 9th – and the strong stresses all on the even syllables – the 2nd, 4th, 6th, 8th and 10th (working out where the stresses are in Shakespeare's speeches is tremendously important to an actor, as we'll see later).

Going back to the two questions again, we know the opening line from Sonnet 18 has ten syllables (or five beats) in it, so it's a line of pentameter. We know that the word *compare* is pronounced iambically (*com-**PARE***), so we can assume the rest of the line is iambically stressed too:

syllables 1st 2nd 3rd 4th   5th 6th   7th 8th   9th 10th
sound   de-**DUM** de-**DUM** de-**DUM** de-**DUM** de-**DUM**
            Shall **I**   com**pare** thee **to** a   **sum**mer's **day**?

Note that an iamb doesn't have to sit over one word, e.g.,

de-**DUM**
mer's **day**

Metrics are driven first and foremost by rhythm, not sense.

When looking at a piece of Shakespeare's poetry, instead of writing *de-**DUM*** over the top of the words, we can just as easily show the weak and strong stresses a different way:

We can use   x   for a weak stress

and   \   for a strong stress.

So now, marked up, the rhythm of a line of iambic pentameter looks like this:

syllables	1st	2nd	3rd	4th	5th	6th	7th	8th	9th	10th
stress	x	\	x	\	x	\	x	\	x	\
sound	de-**DUM**		de-**DUM**		de-**DUM**		de-**DUM**		de-**DUM**	

And with the line from Sonnet 18:

syllables	1st	2nd	3rd	4th	5th	6th	7th	8th	9th	10th
stress	x	\	x	\	x	\	x	\	x	\
	Shall	**I**	com**pare**		thee	**to**	a	**sum**mer's		**day**?

It's worth pointing out that if you were to say these lines in normal conversation, rather than in performance, the stresses might land differently. You could argue that, in terms of the sense of the line, instead of stressing *I* you could stress *shall*, making the *question* more important than the *person* who's asking it, but that would mean stressing words against the rhythm Shakespeare wrote the line in, and, as we'll see in a moment, you need to have an extremely good reason to go against the metre.

I'll repeatedly mention how important it is for an actor to follow the metre – in fact there are rules, or guidelines I should say, for performing such a line of poetry that can help the audience more easily get at its meaning, and we'll come to those guidelines in Act 5.

Just why was iambic pentameter so popular?

In the 1500s the iambic pentameter form exploded onto the public stage. It was being used both on private stages and in the Court from the 1560s – but it was always thought to be too intellectual a style by the general public.

Shakespeare, and his contemporaries, changed that.

Perhaps the reason why iambic pentameter became so popular for playwrights is that

- ⸭ it's what is easy to say in one breath;

- ⸭ therefore it sounds as natural as possible;

- ⸭ therefore we hear something that is essentially human in it: the size of our lungs and the underlying pulse of our bodies is what this verse is built on;

- ⸭ and as far as learning goes, a line of iambic pentameter is within an easy memory span;

- ⸭ therefore the steady recurring rhythm makes it easy to memorise the lines – very useful when you're performing six or seven different plays a week, as Shakespeare's actors would have been doing ...

I think therefore iamb ...

The rhythm that this pairing of syllables makes isn't too dissimilar from your heartbeat. Put your hand on your heart, now, and feel the rhythm it makes. If you're sitting still, and you haven't just been running a marathon, very likely it will be a steady *de-DUM*, *de-DUM*, *de-DUM* about once a second. As we just saw, five of those *de-DUM*s is the rhythm of a line of iambic pentameter.

A not particularly poetic example of iambic pentameter in modern, conversational English would be:

I went to town to buy a coat today
de-**DUM** de-**DUM** de-**DUM** de-**DUM** de-**DUM**

In the English language there are words where a syllable is naturally stronger, where the stress falls on one part and it feels odd to put it on the other: try saying *de-DUM* and put the stress on the *de* – *DE-dum*. It's not so easy. Putting the stress on the *DUM*, on every second syllable, *should* be easier because it's mimicking the natural rhythm of English.

Some say that putting the stress on the non-standard part of a word makes you sound like you're new to the language. In fact, putting the stress on the abnormal part of the word is a very common mistake for someone learning English as a second language: say the word *feather*, and stress the *-er* instead of the *feath-*. It'll sound odd, maybe a bit like someone from France speaking English for the first time: *feath-ER*.

There are some words where you can move the stress around, and it doesn't matter so much. Some people say *re-SEARCH*, others say *RE-search*. *Ad-ver-TISE-ment*, which sounds like American English, and *ad-VER-tise-ment*, which sounds like British English.

Scene 4

A maternity ward

Deciding which word has a strong stress and which has a weak is often very straightforward. The even syllables are strong, the odd are weak. That's quite a structured framework within which to write, and as a result working in that steady metrical rhythm can impose certain things on your writing.

It can make you invent new words to fit the rhythm, and it can make you shorten or lengthen words. It can also affect how you order your words, particularly if you want to make sure a certain word gets a stronger stress.

Vasty is a good example of how Shakespeare invented a new word so as not to upset the flow of the metre. The word *vast* already existed, but in the opening Chorus speech of *Henry V* (lines 11–12) he needed a two-syllable word that expressed the same 'wide-open' quality of *vast* to make the metre work:

\ x \ x \ x \ **x** \ x \
Can this **cockpit hold** the **vasty fields** of **France**?

The rhythm bounces along nicely. He could have used *vast* in its original form:

```
    \   x   \   x   \   x   \   \   x   \
    Can this cockpit hold the vast fields of France?
```

But with two strong stresses together, the rhythm stumbles. If you want a particular word and the sense it conveys, but it hasn't enough syllables, then just make it longer – *vast* becomes *vasty*.

Sometimes the demands of the metre can make you add a syllable in a different way. In this line from *A Midsummer Night's Dream* (Act 2, Scene 1, line 26), you can see how an -*ed* ending is needed to make the rhythm work:

```
    x   \   x   \     x   \     x   \   x   \
    But she perforce withholds the lovèd boy,
```

This occurs hundreds of times in Shakespeare's plays. Play editors often mark an -*ed* ending with an accent, -*èd*, as above, if the metre calls for you to stress it. Stressing the -*ed* keeps the iambic rhythm – it doesn't mean that the -*ed* should be given a particularly strong vocal stress, just that it shouldn't be ignored. To ignore it would do this:

```
    x   \   x   \     x   \     x   \   x
    But she perforce withholds the lov'd boy,
```

Say it out loud, patting the rhythm in the *de-DUM de-DUM* way I explained earlier. The rhythm staggers on *lov'd boy*. Adding the *-ed* ending and making it a two-syllable word – *lov-ed* rather than *lov'd* – keeps the metre regular.

The opposite of this is to remove a syllable and make a *contraction* – shortening a word to fit the metre. For example, contracting *overleaps* to *o'erleaps* (and so changing it from a three-syllable word to a two-syllable word) can have two helpful consequences: it can give a line ten syllables in total rather than eleven (and so keep the metre regular); and it can force the stress of one particular word in a line, rather than another:

```
           x    \    x    \
```
More relative than this. The **play's** the **thing**
```
      x  \  x  \    x  \    x    \  x  \
```
Where**in** I'll **catch** the **con**science **of** the **King**.

This is a straightforward example from *Hamlet* (Act 2, Scene 2, lines 602–3), using similar contractions to ones we still use in speech today. Contracting *play is* to *play's* and *I will* to *I'll* – contracting two-syllable words to one – keeps the lines with ten syllables, and forces stress onto the important words like *catch*, *thing* and *King*. It's a rhyming couplet, too, and making the metre help the rhyme is what it's all about in rhyming couplets.

Without the contractions, things can get a bit stressful

and you have to go for alternative rhythms:

```
              x   \   x  x    \
```
More relative than this. The **play** is the **thing**
```
    x   \ x  x    \   x  \   x    \ x   \
```
Where**in** I will **catch** the **con**science **of** the **King**.

It's technically possible, but it's a less natural, more awkward rhythm.

Contraction is a common trait in modern regular speech
and informal writing, the most obvious example we still
use probably being *o'clock* instead of *o'th'clock* (which in
turn is contracted from *of the clock*) when telling time. Part
of a word or a whole word is removed, letting two (sometimes three) words blend together. They're easy to find in
modern texts of Shakespeare because of the apostrophe.

It's an easy thing to automatically correct, and many
reading Shakespeare out loud for the first time pronounce,
for example, *th'allowance* with four syllables:

```
  \  x  \   x
```
the-a-**llow**-ance

Rather than:

```
  x   \   x
```
tha-**llow**-ance

It's the same rule we discovered earlier when looking at the metrics of a line – if Shakespeare wanted a particular word spoken carefully, he wouldn't contract it. If it's contracted, it should be spoken quickly, and informally, like everyday speech. For example, the first line and a half of a speech from *Macbeth* (Act 1, Scene 7, lines 1–2), marked up, could be read like this:

> x \   x   \   x   x   \   \   x   \
> If **it** were **done** when 'tis **done, then** 'twere **well**
> x   x   \   \   x
> It were **done quick**ly.

The first line wants the attention: it's a healthy line of ten syllables. If Shakespeare hadn't contracted *'tis* and *'twere* (making *it is* and *it were*), it would be a line of twelve syllables.

Shakespeare wanted this a regular line of pentameter – though as you can see from the mark-up, despite the contractions helping to stress the important words like *done*, *well* and *quickly*, it's still not evenly stressed. Why? Perhaps because the two sequences of weak syllables (*when 'tis* and the second *It were*) add pace to the lines – an appropriate effect for someone talking about being in a hurry.

An uneven yet regular line of metre, for a man who is becoming fairly uneven himself, and who is only a scene away from hallucinating a dagger …

If Shakespeare had wanted Macbeth to come onstage and speak slowly and carefully, he'd have written

If it were done when it is done, then it were well

Much more measured and controlled. Contraction brings speed: it makes characters speak faster than they would do if they were spelling out every syllable – a note for the actor, that the character is speaking (and so therefore thinking) quickly or is excited.

Contractions are a part of normal everyday speech, so in using them in his verse, Shakespeare knew that what is normally a very formal style of writing could sound much more colloquial. Not only that, it adds possible character notes for the actors, keeps the pace of the metre up, allows for the stress of particularly important words, and, with the associated informality, brings the audience in closer.

One of the great things about iambic pentameter is that because a strong stress usually falls on the last word of the line of metre, it acts as a vocal springboard into the next line. Try saying the two lines above together, with the stress on *'twere*, instead of *well* as it should be, and you'll see what I mean.

But if you're not an actor, why am I getting you to act this? More to the point, what on earth does all this mean in practical terms, and what good does it do us when reading Shakespeare?

I've a good answer. This very elaborate way of writing poetry, because of the rules that govern it, tells the reader which words to stress when that piece of poetry is being read out loud. Telling the reader which words to stress is, for all intents and purposes, the same as someone directing an actor.

Of course, when you direct an actor, there's more to it than 'which words do you stress'. Sometimes you might want to tell them when to move, where to move to, who to stand close to. Perhaps, if you're feeling particularly inventive in your capacity as director, you might want to start directing the emotions that the text requires your actors to act out.

Shakespeare found a way not only to tell his actors which words to stress, but all the other things too.

This is why I'm taking so much time to explain the fundamentals of poetry, because once it's clear what iambic pentameter actually is in practical terms, we'll discover how Shakespeare directed his actors. This is the key to Shakespeare. Not in *understanding* Shakespeare – I hope I've made it clear that you can understand and enjoy Shakespeare *without* learning these literary terms and conceits – but in *owning* Shakespeare. Because what he did with this very popular style of poetry, this type of metre, was revolutionary.

He turned it on its head, made it do things that other writers didn't, twisted it and played with it and broke every single one of the rules I've just explained to you, improvising like a great jazz player.

Scene 5

Breaking the law at Ronnie Scott's Jazz Club, London

Jazz music came from the blues, which in turn took a lot of its structure from classical music. Dance music, electronica, break-beat, ragga, garage, grunge, house, deep house, hip-hop, trip-hop, ambient trip-hop and countless others – all of them originate from the basic forms that classical music is based on.

Musicians often take an original form and put their own mark on it, changing and developing it into 'something else'. Many musicians do it, but jazz musicians in particular are known for working in this way.

A jazz musician like Miles Davis, or a modern classical musician like Philip Glass, will often play the same section, or riff, of music over and over again, with slight variations every time, making it up as they go along. The slight change will surprise them and you, sometimes make you laugh because you weren't expecting a sudden change, or that note in that place, because everything beforehand led you to expect that after A and B comes C, but the musician gives you Q.

Shakespeare did exactly the same: he learnt the rules of iambic pentameter, then seemed to take great delight in playing around as much as possible with the form. A lot of the reason for all the excitement about this is that although he wasn't the only writer of the time who played with metre in this way, as we'll see in Act 5, the subtleties that came from his playing with it are truly staggering.

A criticism often laid at the door of Christopher Marlowe, one of Shakespeare's contemporaries, is that in his early writing he rarely broke the rules of the metre (the solid structure of iambic pentameter means that once you hit that *de-DUM de DUM* rhythm, you can keep going for hours) and that his characters' speeches would endlessly roll on in straight, regular iambic pentameter:

de-**DUM** de-**DUM** de-**DUM** de-**DUM** de-**DUM**
de-**DUM** de-**DUM** de-**DUM** de-**DUM** de-**DUM**
de-**DUM** de-**DUM** de-**DUM** de-**DUM** de-**DUM**
de-**DUM** de-**DUM** de-**DUM** de-**DUM** de-**DUM**

Looks boring, doesn't it? Some would say it sounds quite boring too. Whether or not this criticism is true, is not our concern. Everyone has to start somewhere. What really crumbles my cookie is what Shakespeare began to do when he got going, and Shakespeare did this: a speech would be rolling along quite innocently …

de-**DUM** de-**DUM** de-**DUM** de-**DUM** de-**DUM**
de-**DUM** de-**DUM** de-**DUM** de-**DUM** de-**DUM**
de-**DUM** de-**DUM** de-**DUM**

Then, of a sudden, Shakespeare would use a word that can *only* be pronounced, or stressed, **STRONG**-weak – **DUM**-de – like ***FEATH**-er*. And the speech would look – or more to the point sound – like this:

de-**DUM** de-**DUM** de-**DUM** de-**DUM** de-**DUM**
de-**DUM** de-**DUM** de-**DUM** de-**DUM** de-**DUM**
de-**DUM** de-**DUM** **DUM**-de

And as a member of the audience you hear those two **DUMS** together and think 'Hang on! What was that? This is the Royal Iambic Pentameter after all! You can't mess with that. I've spent ages learning what that means, you can't change it now I've got the hang of it.' Whatever that character has just said must have been really important to break such an important rule.

And that is exactly what Shakespeare realised.

He could help his actors – and more importantly his audience – and point them towards the important bits, stick a flag in them and say, 'Hey, listen to this, if you remember this later it'll help you understand *why* this character is doing what they're doing.'

I suppose the modern equivalent would be a sudden chord of music in a soap opera, a character, unseen by her husband, turning towards the camera and looking distraught, knowing the child she's carrying isn't really his ...

Here's a piece from *The Taming of the Shrew* (Act 4, Scene 2, lines 2–6) to illustrate the point. Kate's complaining that she's been starved by her new husband:

KATE
The more my wrong, the more his spite appears.
What, did he marry me to famish me?
Beggars that come unto my father's door
Upon entreaty have a present alms,
If not, elsewhere they meet with charity.

Count the syllables of the lines of poetry.

You should find that there are five lines of ten syllables (five lines of pentameter); I do not say five lines of *iambic* pentameter ...

If we were to mark up the first few lines with x and \ they might look like this:

```
 x   \   x   \   x   \   x   \   x   \
```
The more my wrong, the more his spite appears.
```
 x    \  x  \  x  \  x  \  x   \
```
What, did he marry me to famish me?

```
  \   x   x   \   x \ x  \ x    \
  Beggars that come unto my father's door
  x \   x   \ x  \   x \ x    \
  Upon entreaty have a present alms,
  x \   x    \   x    \    x    \ x \
  If not, elsewhere they meet with charity.
```

First of all, the marks back up our pure pentameter claim. There are five x and five \ = ten syllables per line.

Also, Shakespeare has somehow made the most important words like *wrong, spite,* and *marry* even syllables (and so more strongly stressed when spoken), and the less important words like *the* and *to* all odd syllables.

Something else that's interesting: there's one word in the speech which isn't the 'right' way round – to make it clearer I put the first syllable of the word in bold type. If this is pure iambic pentameter, you'd have to say begg-**AR**, stressing the second syllable. But that doesn't sound right. Not only does it not sound right to our ear, the word *beggar* has never been pronounced that way, now or 400 years ago; the stress has always been on the first syllable of the word.

If Shakespeare had wanted the word stressed normally and not upset the metre, he could have written **A** *beggar* … and the metre would force the natural stress of **BEGG**-*ar*.

But he didn't. Putting the word first in the line means

we can't say it iambically as *begg-AR*. He's given the line a
DUM-de opener – a trochee.

Why did he want a trochee *there*? It's the only trochee
in the whole speech …

What if Shakespeare deliberately switched the stress of
the first foot in that sentence from an iamb to a trochee,
forcing a brief change in rhythm and so making the actor
pick the word out from among the rest, to make it clear
how uncomfortable and unusual a thing begging is for
Kate …?

Kate, despite being the *shrew* (= troublesome individual) of the play's title, is a lady of a family with money, and
so the idea of her begging, or even knowing how to beg,
would be ridiculous to her. A complete unknown. And the
trochaic stress emphasises that nicely.

Interesting idea, isn't it?

Now I want to categorically state something here: I'm
not saying Shakespeare was sitting and writing, thinking
'Oh, I'll slip in a nice trochee here, that'll go down well
with my actors, and the audience might notice something
too.' Of course he didn't. Writing this way was as natural to
him as changing TV channels with a remote control is to
you or me. I doubt he ever had to think about it.

That was quite a detailed look at one word in one
speech. To go to the other extreme for a moment, take a
look at this extract from *King Lear*:

LEAR
Why should a Dog, a Horse, a Rat have life,
And thou no breath at all? Thou'lt come no more,
Never, never, never, never, never.
Pray you undo this Button.

> (Act 5, Scene 3, lines 304–7)

This is from right at the end of the play: Lear is dying, his two eldest daughters have died, everything is a mess. Most importantly, his favourite daughter has been hanged, and her body is in his arms.

It's a heartbreaking moment, possibly my favourite moment from the whole canon, for two reasons. The first is that Shakespeare takes Lear from the macro to the micro in the space of two lines – from talking about never seeing his daughter alive ever again, to asking one of his servants to undo a button on his shirt, because he's having trouble breathing.

The second reason I like this moment so much has to do with the metre (surprise, surprise).

Here's one possible reading for these lines:

```
  x    \    x  \   x  \   x \   x   \
Why should a Dog, a Horse, a Rat have life,
  x    \   x    \    x \    x     \    x   \
And thou no breath at all? Thou'lt come no more,
```

```
 \ x  \ x  \ x  \ x  \ x
```
Never, never, never, never, never.
```
 \  x  x \  x  \ x
```
Pray you undo this Button.

We start with two regular lines of iambic pentameter.

We finish with a breathless mix of stresses.

In the middle, we have the same word repeated over and over. Notice though, that it's not iambic (we don't pronounce *never* as *ne-VER*).

In the midst of all the pain, all the anguish, as his heart is breaking – to point out just how entirely screwed up the world at large is, but particularly how torn apart Lear himself is – Shakespeare gives him an entire line of trochaic pentameter in a play (don't forget) that is supposed to be written in iambic pentameter.

Genius.

Never say never again

When you've the strength for it, you're too young, when you've the age, you're too old. It's a bugger, isn't it?

Sir Laurence Olivier, *On Acting* (1986)

Apparently first acted by Richard Burbage – Shakespeare's lead actor, who also first played Hamlet and Othello – playing King Lear has been described as being similar to climbing Everest.

After losing everything, going mad, recovering, then seeing your favourite daughter die, Shakespeare gives you this beautiful line. Sir Robert Stephens, Sir Ian McKellen, Sir Nigel Hawthorne and Sir Ian Holm are a few of the greats to have played this part in recent years, and they all spoke this line completely differently. The sudden shift from iambic pentameter to trochaic nearly always brings a staggering shift in emotion with it, whether the line is whispered, gets louder as it progresses, is shouted, or – well, the options are endless ...

Scene 6

A kitchen: 154 ways to cook an egg

Talking of metrical genius – and ducking aside from the plays for a moment – I need to take a sonnet interlude. Shakespeare wrote 154 sonnets that we know of, and there is a *lot* of academic discussion about them.

The three most common themes are: why did he write them, why did he write so many of them, and what do they mean? In other words, are the sonnets about him and the people he was in love with, or are the characters completely fictional? Again, we're back to trying to divine the man from his work.

There are hundreds of books discussing what the story of the sonnets is, whether the Dark Lady character was a mistress of Shakespeare's, or based on someone he knew (25 of the sonnets are addressed to a woman commonly referred to as the 'Dark Lady'), whether Shakespeare himself is actually one of the characters he writes about, and whether the sonnets reveal his supposed homosexuality.

None of this is important to me. I'm fascinated by what he did with the *metre* in this little canon of work.

He seems to have written most, or at least begun to write them, over a two-year period from 1594 when the plague hit London and the theatres were closed.

Even though he was at the beginning of his writing career, he'd already begun to realise that iambic pentameter can be pretty flexible; that the rules that govern it *are* open to a certain amount of 'negotiation'. Or, as Shakespeare seemed to have decided, a *lot* of negotiation, and his sonnets are a good case in point.

A standard English sonnet is a form of verse strictly consisting of fourteen lines of iambic pentameter. These fourteen lines are traditionally broken up into three sections (known as *stanzas*) of four lines (a stanza of four lines is called a *quatrain*), with six alternating rhymes, followed by a final rhyming couplet!

Confused? It's a whole lot simpler when you look at it like this: a sonnet's rhyme scheme goes

abab cdcd efef gg

The different letters of the alphabet represent different rhymes: *a* rhymes with *a*, *b* with *b*, and so on. Here's Sonnet 18, a classic (and rather famous) *abab cdcd efef gg* sonnet:

quatrain 1

Shall I compare thee to a summer's day?	a
Thou art more lovely and more temperate:	b
Rough winds do shake the darling buds of May,	a
And summer's lease hath all too short a date:	b

quatrain 2

Sometime too hot the eye of heaven shines,	c
And often is his gold complexion dimmed,	d
And every fair from fair sometime declines,	c
By chance or nature's changing course untrimmed:	d

quatrain 3

But thy eternal summer shall not fade,	e
Nor lose possession of that fair thou ow'st;	f
Nor shall Death brag thou wander'st in his shade,	e
When in eternal lines to time thou grow'st:	f

rhyming couplet

So long as men can breathe or eyes can see,	g
So long lives this, and this gives life to thee.	g

It's worth pointing out that *temperate* and *date* would have been pronounced differently, and so rhymed much better in Shakespeare's time, but that small point aside, this is the time-honoured way a normal, conventional English sonnet should go. There's no arguing with it. If you wanna write an English sonnet you write fourteen lines, you write them iambically, and you use the *abab cdcd efef gg* rhyme scheme. End of.

However, of the 154 known sonnets Shakespeare wrote:

§ one of the sonnets doesn't use the standard rhyme scheme: Sonnet 126 has just six rhyming couplets;

§ one (Sonnet 145) is written with four beats per line instead of five, i.e., iambic tetrameter instead of iambic pentameter;

§ one sonnet (20) has eleven syllables in every line. A line of metre with an extra syllable is known as having a *feminine* ending (interestingly, the sonnet is primarily about a woman);

§ only one of the sonnets (150) was written in standard iambic pentameter, i.e., a standard fourteen lines of ten syllables, with only iambic feet.

Think about that for a moment: he's supposed to be writing in iambic pentameter, but as iambic pentameter goes, he plays only one pure song of it (with Sonnet 150) and riffs around the form for the other 153. I'm not going to get into this too deeply, but I'm keen to point out just how much he played around with the style.

A very good friend of mine called Will Sutton, delighted

with his initials one day, learnt all 154 of Shakespeare's sonnets off by heart. As well as being profoundly clever, he has a very good party-piece.

Will thinks that Shakespeare wrote 154 sonnets because that's the maximum number of syllables there can be in a sonnet:

- ⚜ a standard sonnet has fourteen lines of ten syllables = 140 syllables in total;

- ⚜ a sonnet that has a feminine ending on every line has eleven syllables in every line: fourteen lines of eleven syllables = 154 syllables.

There are never more than 154 syllables in any of Shakespeare's sonnets … Why not have 154 mini-experiments in sonnet writing?

It's an interesting idea. Suddenly, this body of work looks like the writing of someone trying to work out exactly what this style of poetry could do. What could it take before it broke? Is it possible, when he's supposed to be writing in iambic pentameter, to take two syllables away from every line – so four strong beats per line instead of five? Well, he has a go with Sonnet 145. Here are the first five lines (I've added a syllable count before each line, and a suggested stress mark-up):

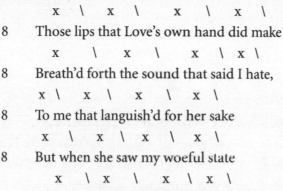

8   Those lips that Love's own hand did make

8   Breath'd forth the sound that said I hate,

8   To me that languish'd for her sake

8   But when she saw my woeful state

8   Straight in her heart did mercy come

It's the only sonnet in the canon written in this metrical form. When Will Sutton performs it, he raps it – and the four-beat, slightly a-rhythmic form does suit a rap beat rather well. You've never heard a Shakespeare sonnet until you've heard it rapped …

The sonnets are important because Shakespeare played with iambic pentameter in exactly the same way in his plays. A lot of the fundamental tricks of the writing trade that Shakespeare played with as a playwright, he seemed to try out first in the sonnets.

We'll never know for sure what his intention was in writing them, but it's clear to me that at least part of his plan was to see how far he could go with the metre, playing and improvising, jazz-like, before launching into the creation of a rather fine canon of work.

Scene 7

An orchestra pit

If you look at all of Shakespeare's plays over the twenty years or so he was writing, you can see that there is a steady change. While the verse in his early plays was a very standard and fairly unsurprisingly solid iambic pentameter, after the theatrical hiatus due to the plague and two years writing sonnets and playing with the metre, his verse becomes more and more complex, and much less predictable. It took him time and practice to hone and learn his craft.

Take a look at this speech from *A Midsummer Night's Dream* (c. 1594), and then one from *Macbeth* (written much later in Shakespeare's career, in 1606):

PUCK
The King doth keep his revels **here tonight**.
Take heed the Queen come not within his sight,
For Oberon is passing fell and wrath
Because that she as her attendant hath
A lovely boy stolen from an **Indian king**.
She never had so sweet a changeling,
And jealous Oberon would have the child

Knight of his train, to trace the **forests wild**.
But she perforce withholds the lovèd boy,
Crowns him with flowers, and makes him all **her joy**.
                              (*A Midsummer Night's Dream*,
                                      Act 2, Scene 2, lines 18–27)

MACBETH
If it were done when 'tis done, then 'twere well
It were **done quickly**. If the assassination
Could trammel up the consequence, and catch
With his surcease success – that but this blow
Might be the be-all and the **end-all!** – here,
But here, upon this bank and shoal of time,
We'd jump the life **to come**. But in these cases
We still have judgement here – that we but teach
Bloody instructions, which, being taught, return
To plague **the inventor**. This even-handed justice
Commends the ingredience of our poisoned chalice
To our **own lips**. He's here in double trust …
                              (*Macbeth*, Act 1, Scene 7, lines 1–12)

Look at where the full stops are in Puck's speech, then look
at where they are in Macbeth's speech; I've made the end
of the sentences bold, to emphasise the point.

As Shakespeare got more sophisticated with his use of
metre, so too did the structure of the lines. Without even
beginning to take either speech apart or look at what any
of it means, a quick glance will show you that the former

is fairly evenly laid out, and the latter kinda all over the place.

If we assume Shakespeare is a grand master of iambic pentameter (and he was), then if he wanted a thought to finish at the end of a line of metre, he could work it so it did. If he didn't, and he made a thought end halfway through a line of metre, he must have done so intentionally.

Following that assumption, if the thoughts are clear and simple, then they'll finish at the end of a line of metre:

The King doth keep his revels here tonight.

is a very good example of that. If we take a thought from Macbeth's speech:

This even-handed justice
Commends the ingredience of our poisoned chalice
To our own lips.

you can see that it spills into three lines of metre, starting and finishing halfway through a metrical line.

If a thought finishing at the end of a metrical line implies clear, simple, straightforward thinking, then a mid-line ending implies hurried, unclear, confused thinking.

Both are great character notes.

A mid-line ending is, essentially, a character interrupting themselves (or being interrupted by others). Halfway through one thought, something else occurs to them, and they go off on a tangent. The speech above from *Macbeth* has a couple of examples of this:

> We'd jump the life **to come**. But in these cases
> We still have judgement here – that we but teach
> Bloody instructions, which, being taught, return
> To plague **the inventor**. This even-handed justice
> Commends the ingredience of our poisoned chalice
> To our **own lips**. He's here in double trust …

Mid-line endings only really start to happen in a more focused way later in Shakespeare's writing, as he got used to what he could do with the metre. Thought and (metrical) line go together in Shakespeare's early writing, as the *Dream* extract shows. Later, the thoughts overwhelm the lines, as in Macbeth's speech.

Shakespeare took this breaking up of the metre further with *shared lines*, where a character's line finishes halfway through a line of metre, and the next character picks up the other half of the metrical line. There's an example immediately after the speech we just looked at from *Macbeth* – again, I've provided a syllable count:

MACBETH

5   Hath he asked for me?

LADY

6–10   Know you not he has?

                          (*Macbeth*, Act 1, Scene 7, line 30)

A line of ten syllables, split evenly, so the actors know that (in order to keep the metre bouncing along nice and regularly) Lady Macbeth should come straight in with her line as soon as Macbeth has spoken his.

We know this to be the case because there are plenty of occasions where Shakespeare doesn't want his actors to immediately come in with their line. In Act 3, Scene 4 of Macbeth, when Macbeth sees Banquo's ghost at the banqueting table, he speaks to the Ghost:

MACBETH

Thou canst not say I did it; never shake
Thy gory locks at me.

ROSS

Gentlemen, rise. His highness is not well.

                    (*Macbeth*, Act 3, Scene 4, lines 49–51)

Ross has a line of ten syllables. Macbeth's first line is a line of ten syllables. The first word in each line is capitalised.

It's definitely in iambic pentameter. Macbeth's second line is only six syllables long, so in order to make sure the regular de-**DUM** de-**DUM** rhythm of the metre isn't thrown out of sync, the actor playing Ross has to wait two beats (marked in bold with **x** and \):

MACBETH
10   Thou canst not say I did it; never shake
    x \ **x** \ **x** \ **x** \ **x** \
6   Thy gory locks at me. _____⌐

ROSS
10   Gentlemen, rise. His highness is not well.

Perhaps Macbeth is entranced, or stunned in fear by the ghost; perhaps Ross is equally transfixed to see his king acting so strangely. Whatever reason the actors give, the two-beat gap in the metre is there, and needs to be filled somehow. More on that in Act 5.

In Shakespeare's earlier writing, these shared lines were mostly used for characters to interrupt each other; in his later writing, he realised he could make it mean much more, and he understood that he could use these metrical nuances to actually orchestrate the pace of a scene.

It was very clear to his actors what he was doing. He was directing them.

Act 5

Enjoy the Play

Scene 1

A London printers, 1622

Here's a question: how do you direct a company of actors if you're dead?

As I touched on earlier, if you're like Shakespeare, you'll leave clues in your writing, a *Da Vinci Code*-like treasure map telling your actors what to do when.

The theatre company Shakespeare worked with, The Lord Chamberlain's Men (later called The King's Men) had been together since 1594; and it was *men* – women weren't allowed to act on stage, so young boy-actors played all the female parts. That company of players carried on working together, apart from a few changes of actors, for most of Shakespeare's writing career, and would have performed over a hundred plays together.

This group would have known each other incredibly well, and understood how each other worked intimately. As would Shakespeare: when he wrote his plays, he wrote them knowing *his* actors would be performing them, so he wrote for *them* as much as he did for his audience.

A writer watching [his own work] *wants to see the actors relishing the language.*

Harold Pinter, *Working With Pinter*, 2007

This flexibility in his writing is clear from the way Shakespeare's clown character changed over the course of his writing. William Kemp was the clown with The Chamberlain's Men – and so Shakespeare's main clown – from 1594 to 1599, and was the first to play Dogberry in *Much Ado About Nothing*. Robert Armin took over from Kemp as the company's clown in 1599, and was the first Feste in *Twelfth Night*.

It seems that Kemp was a gifted comic, and Armin much more of a singer, so following the change in cast, the clown character in the plays noticeably shifted from a wordy slapstick-clown to the more solemn, singing, melancholic-clown: the writer following the actor's individual personality.

Scene 2

A graveyard

Had Shakespeare been interested in fame beyond death, he might have done something to make sure his plays survived him. Ben Jonson oversaw the printing of his own collected works in 1616, but Shakespeare did nothing to help his own writing live on.

Fortunately, as we saw in Act 1, his actors saw fit to preserve the works, and thank goodness they did. Thanks, not just because we now have the plays, but because, with the arrival of the Puritans' rule of the land soon after Shakespeare died, there is now a 40-year hole in theatre history.

Working back from the 20th century, we have actors who've worked with actors who've worked with actors and so on, right back to the Restoration period, in 1660. Acting techniques passed on and on.

Before 1660? Nothing. Almost all the acting traditions from Shakespeare's time are lost. There are tales of actors from 1660 who could remember contemporaries of Shakespeare, but the lessons that were passed down from actor to actor in Shakespeare's time were lost when Civil War broke out in 1642. England became a Commonwealth and the Puritan Parliament, desperate to maintain control of the people, issued an ordinance suppressing all stage plays: theatre, the use of fine clothes and 'flippant' behaviour – all obviously great sins in the eyes of the Puritans – were banned. Soon afterwards, the Globe was torn down.

The Puritans followed up that little *coup de grace* with an order in 1647 stating that *all* theatres were to be destroyed, all actors to be arrested and flogged, and anyone caught trying to see a play to be fined. The art, the style and the techniques that Shakespeare wrote for and, likewise, the writing that his actors acted, were being forgotten, and were nearly lost forever.

Nearly. A few years before theatre – and Christmas – was banned, two of Shakespeare's lead actors thought it might be time to remember their old dead chum Will in style. So what if *he* never showed any interest in having his plays printed up ...

Plus, it might make a few quid.

The First Folio of 1623 ... Using the clues that Shakespeare wrote into the First Folio, it's possible to work out, or at least get an idea of, how Shakespeare's company worked. The Folio is the closest thing we have to Shakespeare. Although it was printed seven years after his death, it was edited by Henry Condell and John Hemmings, two of his lead actors who would have worked very closely with him. If anyone would know how his plays should be printed, it would be the people who had acted in them.

I know actors who swear by it, and I know actors who don't know what it is. The First Folio is a number of things, and at first glance it can seem rather daunting.

It's not like any book you'll be used to. It's big, it's heavy, and the page numbering is all over the place. There are online versions of the Folio text that are slightly more user-friendly, but then there are still the unusual spellings and typeface to deal with.

Why bother using it, then, when I have very handy, portable, modern editions of Shakespeare's plays scattered around my house?

The Folio edition of the plays, while far from perfect, is the closest thing we have to the plays as Shakespeare intended, and if anyone questions its worth, I always come back to this basic argument: Shakespeare wrote his plays for his actors, and this is the only version of the plays they had a hand in.

Folio, The First ...

There were about 1,000 copies printed of the First Folio of 1623, and about 229 of those survive today, having somehow lived through the regime of the Puritans, the Great Fire of London (to which it is thought many copies of plays, manuscripts, etc., were lost) and three more centuries of life. Copies have been found dusty on shelves of libraries, and mouldy in attics in northern England. Seventy-nine copies live in the Folger Library in Washington. Copies rarely come up for sale, and when they do, they sell for millions.

The First Folio had four reprints in the 17th century:

§   The Second Folio of 1632, with minor corrections added;

§   The Third Folio of 1663, with minor corrections – and some new errors! – added;

§   The Third Folio, second impression, of 1664 – the rarest of Folios, as many copies were destroyed in the Great Fire of 1666. Seven plays were added to the 36 extant, most of which are considered not to have been written by Shakespeare;

§   The Fourth Folio of 1685, which was essentially a reprint of the Third Folio, with more corrections and errors added.

It's a rare and very valuable book. Go on, go and check those bookshelves and attics ...

Scene 3

Backstage at Shakespeare's Globe, 1599

A play would rarely be found all in one place before the First Folio was printed. The actors would have their parts written out on separate rolls of paper (scrolls), with the three cue words of whoever was speaking before them written above their speeches. Due to the frequency of new plays and the short rehearsal time, they probably didn't have much time to find out what was going to happen next, how the play ended, or who was playing which part ...

There was a *platt* (a piece of paper with a hole in the middle, through which it was nailed up backstage) which detailed the order of the scenes, the fights and dances, the exits and entrances that took place, and all the doubling up of parts that the boy-actors would take care of, all switching hats and costumes as fast as possible.

The scripts were handed out this way because it would be time-consuming and costly to write out the entire play for every actor. Also, by making sure that entire copies of the plays were scarce, the theatre company limited the chances of rival companies stealing their brand-new product.

The actors' cue-scripts were copied from the prompt-copy of the play, held by Edward Knight, the Book-keeper of the company, who would have ensured that any cuts or changes made by the acting company or the Master of the Revels would be copied down and followed. Some say the actors copied out their own parts, which would undoubtedly help them to learn their parts quickly.

So the scripts – what we now know as literary texts – really were solely and simply the tools of actors. The complete prompt-copies or, if they couldn't be found, the actors' cue-scripts were what Condell and Hemmings used to put the First Folio together.

They obviously couldn't ask Shakespeare how he would want the plays presented, so it's likely they printed the plays as *they* would want to use them. Note I say *use* not *read*. They were the equivalent of plumbers organising a tool-box. A plumber's tool box would not be for looking at, it would be for using. *This is a book of how to act William Shakespeare's plays*, is what they'd have been thinking.

There are a number of clues in the Folio that show an actor where, for instance, they should stand on the stage. Whether they should speak quickly or slowly. Which words they should carefully stress because those particular words are crucial to the story-telling (as an Elizabethan actor wouldn't have been able to read the whole play, how would he know otherwise?). I'll go through some of these clues shortly.

Now the reason I suggest you go to the First Folio when looking at a speech or scene or a play of Shakespeare's is because a lot of the modern editions have edited these clues out. Modern editors, over the years, forgetting these are actor's tools and thinking of the plays only as literary works, have tried to neaten the texts up a bit.

When preparing a Shakespeare play for publication, modern editors will go back to the Folio and the Quarto versions, and decide which punctuation is right, and which is wrong. They'll add exclamation marks to try to make a character's intention clearer. They'll remove the capitalisations of words in the middle of a sentence – because that's not how we write now, or because it appears to be random and without meaning.

All of which is completely understandable: the written language hadn't begun to standardise in Shakespeare's time, and it would be easy to mistake these clues for errors. And certainly we know that the Folio typesetters introduced many errors when the First Folio was being printed. There were five 'Hands' involved – five different compositors – evidently of varying intellects and each with their own idiosyncratic way of spelling, so despite being as close as we can get to Shakespeare, the Folio is by no means flawless.

But modern editors are not actors, and they will remove or replace words, add full stops in the middle of thoughts, or change prose to verse (Mercutio's 'Queen Mab' speech in *Romeo and Juliet* is a good example of that) because the text as it stands doesn't seem to make sense.

The thing is, sometimes a particularly odd turn of phrase won't make any sense at all unless it's spoken on stage in front of an audience, no matter how much editing work is put into it.

Modern editors – and modern productions, for that matter – are also prone to cutting, and before removing something from a Shakespeare play, it's worth going to fairly extreme lengths to find out why it was there in the first place.

I always work from the assumption that Shakespeare is right more often than not, brilliant playwright that he was, and knew more about drama than I do. If something doesn't make sense I'll work at it, and work at it again. I'll go away, think about it, work at it again, *then* question whether it might just be bad writing. It's too easy to cut or rewrite something because it doesn't make sense immediately.

Even if it's a quick look, I always find it's worth at least *comparing* the Folio with a modern edition, to see what I might be losing. And even if this system is a haphazard accident of typesetters – *it still works.*

Take a look at a speech from *Titus Andronicus.* The Goth is describing how he discovers Aaron the Moor talking to his baby, and how he captures them both (the bold type marks out the end of a thought):

Penguin edition

Second Goth

Renowned Lucius from our troops I strayed
To gaze upon a ruinous monastery,
And as I earnestly did fix mine eye
Upon the wasted building, suddenly
I hear a child cry **underneath a wall**.
I made unto the noise, when soon I heard
The crying babe controlled with this discourse:
'Peace, tawny slave, half me and **half thy dam**!
Did not thy hue bewray whose brat thou art,
Had nature lent thee but thy mother's look,
Villain, thou mightst have **been an emperor**.
But where the bull and cow are both milk-white,
They never do beget a **coal-black calf**.
Peace, villain, **peace**!' – even thus he rates the babe –
'For I must bear thee to a trusty Goth
Who, when he knows thou art the Empress' babe,
Will hold thee dearly for **thy mother's sake**.'
With this my weapon drawn, I rushed upon him,
Surprised him suddenly, and brought him hither
To use as you think needful **of the man**.

Folio edition

Goth.

Renowned *Lucius*, from our troups I straid,
To gaze vpon a ruinous Monasterie,
And as I earnestly did fixe mine eye
Vpon the wasted building, suddainely
I heard a childe cry vnderneath a wall:
I made vnto the noyse, when soone I heard,
The crying babe control'd with this discourse:
Peace Tawny slaue, halfe me, and halfe thy Dam,
Did not thy Hue bewray whose **brat thou art**?
Had nature lent thee, but thy Mothers looke,
Villaine thou might'st haue bene an **Emperour**.
But where the Bull and Cow are both milk-white,
They neuer do beget a cole-blacke-Calfe:
Peace, villaine peace, euen thus he rates the babe,
For I must beare thee to a trusty Goth,
Who when he knowes thou art the Empresse babe,
Will hold thee dearely for **thy Mothers sake**.
With this, my weapon drawne I rusht vpon him,
Surpriz'd him suddainely, and brought him hither
To vse, as you thinke needefull **of the man**.

(*Titus Andronicus*, Act 5, Scene 1, lines 20–39)

The capital letters are probably the first things that will
jump out at you as being different – and, rather handily, a
quick glance at them will give you an idea of what the
speech is all about:

Lucius	who the Goth is talking to
Monasterie	a place
Tawny	a colour
Dam	mother
Hue	reference to a colour
Mothers	mother
(thou mightst have bene) an Emperour	prediction of future
Bull and Cow (are both milk-white)	reference to colour
Coal-blacke-Calfe	reference to colour
Goth	reference to Aaron's alliance
the Empresse babe	reference to the baby's mother
thy Mothers sake	reference to the baby's mother

These capital letters tell us who the Goth is talking to, where he was when he found Aaron, a number of descriptive words about Aaron's baby, and Aaron's main concerns – the mother and the Emperor. By this point in the play we know the child is illegitimate, that the Empress and Aaron have been having an affair behind the Emperor's back, and that the colour of the babe's skin would make it clear who the real father was …

But if you didn't know all this plot information – as

indeed the actor in Shakespeare's time speaking the speech most likely wouldn't, not having read the whole play – but you are used to your writer's style, a quick scan of the speech tells the whole story.

Every capitalised word except *Lucius* and *Goth* is lost from the Penguin edition.

Also, the way the speeches are presented to you is quite different in the two editions. The Penguin version has six thoughts, and two exclamation marks, whereas the Folio has four thoughts, and one question mark. It may seem pedantic, but full stops and exclamation marks are pretty demanding things, and very hard not to follow. The extra full stops in the Penguin version break the speech up a lot more and halt the flow, and exclamation marks all too often get interpreted as 'time to shout'.

The Folio version flows more, and is less measured – more a breathless account of a foot soldier than a piece of classical poetry.

Actors often don't like being told how to say a line by anyone other than the writer or the director. If writers want a word or a sentence exclaimed, they'll probably add an exclamation mark. If they don't, they won't. How can Shakespeare editors – fine, upstanding people though they are – have any idea about whether a line should be exclaimed or not, when it can take weeks for a modern actor to decide how to deliver a line?

All that said, we need modern editions, and they're bloody useful. For one thing, the metre is laid out as it should be (I'll show you what I mean by that in a moment), and, unsurprisingly, that gets my vote.

Going to the Folio – which, as my Father the Linguist would be quick to point out, is (a) far from reliable and (b) has punctuation and spelling that was far from standardised; and so (c) to rely on the placing of a comma would be foolhardy – is still, in my mind, going as far back and getting as close to Shakespeare's intention as we ever will. It wipes the canvas of the text as clean as possible, without modern interpretations forced on us. The Royal Shakespeare Company seems to agree: their latest edition of the plays, despite making some editorial changes and additions, attempts to follow the Folio texts throughout.

Another reason why I like and recommend it so much is that the Folio spelling reminds you how *olde* the texts are, which reminds you of the world they were written in, and so keeps more of an Elizabethan head on your shoulders.

In Act 1 we looked at why a general idea of the Elizabethan life and theatrical context was important in getting to grips with Shakespeare; now we'll see just how vital a little bit of background knowledge can be, when we take a look at Shakespeare's hidden clues to his actors.

Shockingly exclaimed ...!

A great example of the changes modern editors make is in Patrick Tucker's *Secrets of Acting Shakespeare*. Tucker uses lines of Romeo's from *Romeo and Juliet* (Act 5, Scene 1, lines 22–4), providing all the Elizabethan versions. Romeo has just been told (inaccurately, as it turns out) that Juliet, his love, has died:

> *First Quarto (1597)*
> Pardon me Sir, that am the Messenger of such bad tidings.
> Rom: Is it euen so? Then I defie my Starres.

> *Second Quarto (1599)*
> O Pardon me for bringing these ill newes,
> Since you did leave it for my office Sir.
> Rom. Is it euen so?
> Then I denie you Starres.

> *First Folio (1623)*
> O pardon me for bringing these ill newes,
> Since you did leave it for my office sir.
> Rom. Is it in so?
> Then I denie you starres.

Now, putting on the hat of a modern editor, you can see it would be hard to work out which version of the line Shakespeare intended. The interesting thing, though, as Tucker points out, is that none of the modern editors choose any of the lines handed down from the Elizabethans in their entirety, rather choosing to amalgamate the lines, and (surprise surprise) most adding an exclamation mark for good effect.   (cont.)

Kittredge (1940):	Is it e'en so? Then I defy you, stars!
Riverside (1974):	Is it e'en so? Then I defy you, stars!
Arden (1979):	Is it e'en so? Then I defy you, stars!
Oxford (1986):	Is it e'en so? Then I defy you, stars.

This is just one example of the changes modern editors make. It's right to try to make more sense of the line, but one of the meanings of *denie* in Elizabethan times was *renounce*; the *starres* were *fate* or *destiny*. So the Folio and Second Quarto versions *do* make sense as they are.

As for the added exclamation mark, well, at this moment, Romeo could be crying, screaming, or speaking softly, but the added mark doesn't leave very much room for interpretation ...

Scene 4

Brooklyn, 1990

When you're faced with having to analyse, write about, or simply just enjoy a piece of Shakespeare that you don't know, it can seem like a daunting task. So to take things to the other extreme for a moment, have a read through the song extract below:

High flyin like the Millennium Falcon, piloted by Han Solo
I never roll for dolo, frontin on me's a no-no
Understand? Doin this for my family
Ha ha, check it out y'all
Yo I'm tryin to make a dollar out of what makes sense
Add it up, told my daddy I'd be a rich man
You never know when your fate gon' switch hand
Get today's solid ground out of yesterday's quicksand
I was a young boy – who dreamt about being a big man
on small looseleaf sheets I sketched a big plan
Gotta handle business properly, boost up my economy
Store it up and get my mom some waterfront property
Yesterday was not for me but nowaday it's time for me
The streets is watchin me, I watch back, that's the policy
Movin along my oddesey like blood through the artery
Navigate the treacherous and make it seem effortless

Let those who make the exodus seekin the North beacon
from beatin and hog-eatin, from punishment all season
from hands cracked and bleedin – cotton thorns in your palms
It's for y'all that I sketch these songs, and it goes.
Yea though I walk through the valley of the shadow
I fear no man, because faith is the arrow
My vocal chord travel worldwide to block narrow
We can blow with the ammo or go mano-a-mano
Kweli is you wit me? (Whattup whattup?) Let's make it happen
I *BURN* through your argument with action
My eyes stay fastened to tomorrow lookin for a brighter day
When y'all wanna leave y'all? Right away …

'Know That', by Brooklyn hip-hop artist and actor Mos Def

§ The most obvious thing to say about it is that it's written like poetry, with capital letters at the start of most lines. Not to mention the rolling rhymes – *shadow-arrow-narrow-mano*, *effortless-exodus*, *beacon-beatin-eatin-bleedin*.

§ There are some odd words (*dolo*, *hog-eatin*), and some different spellings (*nowaday* is missing its final -*s*, *bleedin*, *beatin* and a few others are missin their final -*g*).

§ There's some good language play: *dollar* and *sense* (cents), *store it up* and *property* (*store* as in *save* as well as in *shop*), *North beacon* rhyming with *beatin* and *hog-eatin*, making *beacon* remind you of 'bacon', *beatin* and *hog-eatin* backing up that idea. There's some Spanish, too, with *mano-a-mano*.

§ Plus there's a pretty good cultural reference, Han Solo and the Millennium Falcon, from the film *Star Wars* (1977), and a Bible reference:

Yea though I walk through the valley of the shadow
                                                    (Psalm 23, Verse 4)

Poetry, unusual words, language play, and cultural references: there's doubtless a lot more to find, and this is no renowned literary work from hundreds of years ago, it's a great but fairly regular and relatively unknown rap song from the 1990s.

This song isn't actually much different from Shakespeare and the kind of things you'll find in his plays. Go to the back of a Penguin edition of Shakespeare (or look below the text in an Arden or Cambridge edition) and you'll find that the editor has pointed out all the Bible references and the cultural references, named the stories Shakespeare based his writing on, explained any use of foreign languages, and discussed particular pieces of language play.

In this Act I'm going to use part of a scene from one of the most frequently performed plays in Shakespeare's canon, *Macbeth*, and take it apart. The techniques I'll use are exactly the same as the ones I used to look at Mos Def's lyrics, but supported by the important bits and pieces I've talked about in the previous Acts: the context, the story, the characters, the settings, and the thoughts, and how they're *all* expressed through the language and metre.

Once I've shown how to do it with this scene, you can use the same techniques and tools to break open any Shakespeare scene you encounter.

It's William back from the dead,
But I rap bout gats and I'm black instead,
It's Shakespeare, reincarnated
I'm similar to William, but a little different,
I do it for kids that's illiterate, not Elizabeth,
My thing, I tell em like this
It's like Shakespeare, with a little twist

Modern American hip-hop is complete garbage: it's about champagne and naked women, so rap has not got respect as an intellectual entity ... Great rappers like Chuck D are literary geniuses; they're no different from Shakespeare, Blake or Roald Dahl.

Akala, winner of the Best Hip-Hop Artist 2006,
Music of Black Origin (Mobo) Awards
(quoted in *The Guardian*, September 2006; above, lyrics
from the Radio Edit of his song 'Shakespeare')

Scene 5

London, England, 1600s

So why have I chosen an extract from *Macbeth* rather than any other play? No particular reason, as it goes, although it's one of the most studied plays, so a lot of people have a memory of the play being particularly dull, which it really isn't – Macbeth is Al Pacino in *Scarface* (1983).

One might equally ask why did Shakespeare choose to write it in the first place, and then we're back to the basics: context. A bit like understanding the finer points of iambic pentameter, dig into a little bit of the play's background, and it'll make the rest of it much easier to crack.

When Shakespeare wrote *Macbeth* (around 1605), Galileo was still five years away from announcing that the sun *didn't* go round the Earth, and the previous few years of Shakespeare's (and everyone else's) life in England had been fairly traumatic.

Will's dad had died in 1601, and the following year while writing *Hamlet* (a play primarily to do with the grief of losing a father), it seems that Shakespeare started to think about his own future, and bought some land and a cottage in his home town of Stratford-upon-Avon.

The next year, 1603, not so long after Shakespeare had

performed before her, his patron, the monarch of England, Queen Elizabeth I, died.

This, in and of itself, needs to be seen in the context of the time.

The effect that the death of a monarch would have had on the Elizabethans would have been monumental. The closest equivalent we might have would probably be the death of Princess Diana in 1997, or the assassination of JFK in 1963. Anyone old enough will remember the world stopping, the grief, the masses pulling together in support.

Imagine (or remember) that, and then magnify it 100 times over.

Why would such an event be so devastating? Well, it was an incredibly religious time. The two main religions of England were Catholicism and Protestantism. Queen Elizabeth was Protestant, but unlike her predecessors was more relaxed about people practising Catholicism, i.e., they wouldn't be tortured or executed as long as they didn't threaten the realm or her reign.

The king or queen in Shakespeare's time was considered to be one step down from God. God would speak through the monarch. The monarch was leader, protector, father, mother, and the route to heaven. Love and obey your monarch, and you will go to heaven. Conversely, defy, contradict or kill a king and you are killing God, and you will surely go to hell.

Disloyalty to one's nation is treason, and to plot against the monarch was high treason, one of the most serious crimes the Elizabethans had at their disposal. If you were caught committing an act of treason you were branded as a traitor (in Dante's *Inferno* the lowest and worst circle of hell was reserved for traitors), and you would very probably be sentenced to death.

Most likely (if you've seen the end of Mel Gibson's 1995 film *Braveheart* you'll be familiar with this process), death would involve you being hung by the neck until you were nearly dead, then your insides would be drawn out of you while you were still alive, then your body would be quartered (as the name suggests, cut into four pieces) and sent to the four corners of the kingdom. Your head would be put on a spike and displayed at the, ahem, head of London Bridge, and would be the first thing people would see when entering London from the south – as a message to all others considering betrayal. Unless you were a woman, in which case you'd just be burnt at the stake.

The closest parallel we have occurred in March 2007, when a Swiss man appeared in a Thai court after being accused of insulting the Thai king (still considered by many Thais to be semi-divine) by spray-painting images of him. He was looking at a *75-year* jail sentence. For graffiti. He was later sentenced to a mere ten years in prison, and then the king, 'in his kindness', pardoned him …

Pretty persuasive message.

Back to the context: Queen Elizabeth I dies, and the crown goes to King James VI of Scotland, who becomes King James I of England too. Now as anyone knows who has been to school in Britain or seen *Braveheart*, there's a fairly unhappy history between the Scots and the English, mainly due to the English trying to claim Scotland as their own, and the Scots wanting none of it.

After centuries of animosity, there was now a Scottish king on the English throne.

What Shakespeare thought of all this is a moot point, but it's worth noting that while all this was going on in London, his personal life was about to take a kicking. Back in his home town of Stratford, where he was setting up his retirement nest, all theatrical performances of any kind were summarily banned by a puritanically-minded town council.

Betrayed by his own, some might say. In buying the cottage and land, it would appear he'd just started to think about returning home and settling down, and now his life's work was essentially barred from taking place there. Think Elvis coming home to Memphis and being told that rock and roll music was forbidden.

The next year, 1604, James comes to London and is crowned King of England, and if that didn't piss on a number of English loyalists' chips, then the fact that one of the first things he did was condemn tobacco, everyone's new and favourite import from the Americas, certainly upset a few more.

Elizabeth I had had her fair share of rebels, treasonists and revolters, yet despite the fact that the unrest was reaching bubbling point, no one had so far tried to do what Guy Fawkes and his mates would try to do to James: a conspiracy commonly known as the Gunpowder Plot – an attempt to blow up the Houses of Parliament, and kill the king.

It failed, of course, and around the time that James had Guy Fawkes and his fellow conspirators put to death for treason, Shakespeare was putting the finishing touches to his new play.

Revenge, in Jacobean times

James's reign as king began with £350,000-worth of debt from Elizabeth's reign and an assassination attempt, and ended with an outbreak of bubonic plague. Elizabeth had been a strong, fighting queen; James was a king from another country, afflicted with a number of illnesses, including a rather crippling arthritis. It was a time of great change and turmoil, and during these troubled, early years of James's sovereignty, Shakespeare wrote (among others) *The Winter's Tale*, *Macbeth* and *King Lear*, thought by many to be his greatest and most thought-provoking tragedies.

Hamlet, generally considered to be his best work, is Shakespeare's only Revenge Tragedy – a particular type of tragedy that was extremely popular at the time. Now fairly infamous, the

Jacobean Revenge Tragedies seemed to especially capture the Elizabethans' imaginations. *Hamlet* is certainly one (despite being written a few years before James came to the throne, and so technically Elizabethan and not Jacobean), together with *The Spanish Tragedy* by Thomas Kyd, one of Shakespeare's contemporaries, and the anonymously written *Revenger's Tragedy*.

Elements that a standard Revenge Tragedy tended to include were: murder, ghosts, real or feigned madness, and a great scene of violence towards the end of the play, culminating in the death of most of the characters. The main theme was usually the corruption of power within monarchy, and the plot often involved an attempt by a protagonist to restore equilibrium within the state by removing a usurping ruler (Shakespeare's *Julius Caesar*, where the ruler is murdered by a group of conspiring senators, was written at a similar time).

Perhaps the Elizabethan – now Jacobean – people found a release by watching these tragedies: taking part, for a few hours, in acts of revenge, rebellion and blood-letting; and so venting what anger and dissatisfaction they might have had with the state in the safety of a wooden theatre, leaving behind only their ire and a stage covered in pig's blood ...

Playwrights, like their audiences, want to explore aspects of life they hope they'll never experience, as much as they want to explore life they have experienced.

Shakespeare had written about the loss of a father in *Hamlet*. He then wrote about the loss of a monarch in *Measure for Measure, All's Well That Ends Well, Timon of Athens* (though Timon is less a monarch, more a monarchic figure), and *King Lear*, and every time he wrote it from a different angle, choosing a different take on the idea, perhaps in response to the world around him: while Elizabeth was dying, while she died, while the crown shifted to Scotland and the future lay uncertain, then while James assumed the throne.

It's a theme he carried on exploring until he stopped writing – what happens when you take a powerful man, and then take his power away from him?

When the Gunpowder Plot was uncovered, suddenly the unthinkable was put before Shakespeare; something he'd written about earlier with his *Henry VI* trilogy, but probably not something he ever thought he'd be able to practically witness at first hand. A fantastic, fascinating idea for a play:

What would it be like to kill a king?
What would it be like to kill *God*?
And get away with it?
And in so doing, become king …
… You could *become* God.

These were terrible, treasonous thoughts, and only a slight dramatic extension beyond the bloody reality that Fawkes and his fellows had been planning.

In the midst of a dying monarch he knew and loved,

in the midst of a strange, new and uncertain monarch (would James be a good or an evil king?), and while civil unrest was so strong it had almost reached anarchy – in the midst of all this, Shakespeare wrote a new play.

A dark and enigmatic thriller about treason, murder, a kingdom in chaos, forecasts of a doomed future, and betrayal of friends.

He wrote *Macbeth*.

Scene 6

The mind of an Elizabethan, 1605

*M*acbeth isn't a literary text, it's a bloody, vicious, scary, turn-the-world-upside-down-and-shake-it-by-the-neck thriller! It really is similar to Al Pacino's journey in the film *Scarface* – a man told he will be king, who kills everyone in his way, achieves his goal, becomes paranoid, trusts no one, and is eventually brought down.

It's the only play of Shakespeare's that is known world-wide to have a curse on it. I know a lot of people who insist that in their day-to-day lives they are not superstitious in the slightest, and yet will categorically NOT speak the name of the play, or its lead character. *Macbeth* is more commonly known in the theatrical world as 'The Scottish Play'. Even *I* am loath to say it on stage, and I know people who get really upset if you don't observe the rules that surround The Curse.

While many of Shakespeare's plays provoke boredom in people who don't know his work, *Macbeth* seems to cause a certain amount of trepidation. Not without fair reason, too. It has witches, ghosts, blood, death, revenge, confusion, horses eating each other (I'm serious), and worse than all that, The Killing of a King.

The Curse of *Macbeth*

It's held to be incredibly bad luck to mention the name 'Macbeth' outside of rehearsal rooms or while the play is being performed. Many people in the profession refuse to call it by its chosen name, preferring 'The Scottish Play'. But why? Productions have suffered from their actors dying or being injured. King James banned the play for five years after seeing it, perhaps because (as an author of a work on witchcraft) the witches' incantations were too real for comfort.

There are more down-to-earth reasons:

§ There's a great deal of violent action in it, often taking place in the dark, which makes it more likely that accidents will happen.

§ It's also the shortest tragedy Shakespeare wrote, making it cheaper to put on – which has led to the theory that theatre companies having a difficult financial time would mount a production to make money fast, and perhaps cut corners when it came to rehearsals and safety.

§ And of course it's now a self-fulfilling prophecy: actors expect something to go wrong and, unwittingly, make it happen.

Lifting the Curse ...

If someone does say 'Macbeth' outside of performance or rehearsal, there are a number of cures to the curse. Here are two:

§ Leave the room or space you are in, close the door behind you. Turn around three times, swear, knock on the door, and ask to be let back in.

  🖐 If there's no time for all of that, quoting Hamlet's line, 'Angels and ministers of grace defend us!' (Act 1, Scene 4) will do it.

Superstitious?

Some productions that have felt the curse ...

  🖐 During the play's first performance, Hal Berridge, the boy playing Lady Macbeth, died backstage, and (tradition says) Shakespeare had to play the part.

  🖐 In a production in Amsterdam in 1672, the actor playing Macbeth used a real dagger, and killed the actor playing Duncan in front of the audience.

  🖐 During rival performances of the same play in New York in 1849, a riot broke out and over twenty people died.

  🖐 In John Gielgud's 1942 production, three actors died Duncan, and two of the witches – and the set designer committed suicide.

  🖐 Cambridge Shakespeare Company, 2001: Macduff injured his back, Lady Macbeth hit her head, Ross broke his toe, and two cedar trees crashed to the ground, destroying the set.

There's a really important scene (Act 2, Scene 4) soon after Macbeth has murdered King Duncan, where an Old Man meets Ross and they discuss the repercussions of the king's death. The scene is often cut in modern productions, but it's fantastically important. The first thing the Old Man (Shakespeare was never too worried about names) says is:

Threescore and ten I can remember well;
Within the volume of which time I have seen
Hours dreadful and things strange; but this sore night
Hath trifled former knowings.

(*Macbeth*, Act 2, Scene 4, lines 1–4)

Ross mentions that it's so dark during the daytime it seems like night. The Old Man replies with a story of a falcon being killed by an owl (if at all, the norm would be the other way round), and before Macduff enters to talk about what will happen next, the Old Man and Ross speak of Duncan's horses growing so crazed that they burst from their stables and then *ate* each other …

The picture that is conjured up is of a stormy, dark, tempestuous and chaotic land, where nothing is as it should be. A land without a king. A land without God.

Add to this melting pot of fear, murder and mayhem the Elizabethans' aforementioned somewhat muscular ability to suspend their disbelief, and you have yourself quite a concoction. Remember: death on stage would have been a different spectacle to witness for them. When they saw someone die on stage, then as far as they were concerned, that person really died.

As it happens, not too many people die on stage in *Macbeth* – Duncan, Lady Macbeth, and Macbeth all die off-stage. Perhaps Shakespeare wrote it this way for the very reason that the audience would get too scared; or perhaps because the general subject-matter of the play was hard enough for the audience to deal with – you can *talk* about the death of a Scottish king, but maybe *showing* it might have put Shakespeare slightly too close to the edges of treason, or give the Master of the Revels too much to complain about.

The Master of the Revels was an immensely powerful man. No play could be performed at Court – where the monarch would be entertained – without his authorisation, and by 1606 he was given control over the plays performed in the public theatres too. The aim was to ensure that the Court received the best possible entertainment, and that no one would be upset too greatly by anything they saw.

Considering recent events, parts of *Macbeth* might have made the audience a little too uncomfortable, seeing as they'd have been watching the play in the aftermath of the Gunpowder Plot, and perhaps only a short time before Guy Fawkes was to be executed, so Shakespeare would have to be very careful with his phrasing.

But death, murder, and treason aren't the only fun bits in the play. We've also got witches. The play opens with a scene where three witches are incanting a spell, in the middle of a storm of thunder and lightning. This is incredibly important too, and needs contextualising almost as much as the death of a monarch did. Unlike today's productions of *Macbeth*, the witches in Shakespeare's production would probably have caused quite a ruckus, as the Elizabethans would have been watching these scenes in the middle of the European Witch Craze.

The witch-hunts that formed much of the European Witch Craze took place over 400 years, from towards the end of the 13th century to the mid-17th century. England was swept up in the furore too, and the Witchcraft Act of 1541, passed under Henry VIII, stated: 'It shall be Felony to practise, or cause to be practised Conjuration, Witch-craft, Enchantment or Sorcery.'

The years of the Witch Craze would have been terrifying for people. Fear of witches still abounded in Shakespeare's time, and far beyond it.

In 1616, the year Shakespeare died, Johannes Kepler, a German mathematician and a close friend to the Emperor, only *just* managed to save his mother from being burnt at the stake for being a witch, by using the clout he had in the Court. Eighty-six years after Shakespeare wrote *Macbeth*, the Salem witch trials took place (made famous in modern theatre by Arthur Miller's play *The Crucible*).

The witch hunts would have been truly terrifying.

If anybody thought you might be a witch, you would be put under trial, often involving extremely horrible meth-ods of torture, until you either confessed (and were then burnt at the stake while still alive) or you died from the torture. If you cried or were seen to be afraid during the trial, it was a sign you were a witch. If you knew or were kin to a witch, you would be put under trial as a suspected witch. The examiner could look for a diabolical mark on your body, like a birthmark or mole, which was a sure sign you were a witch; if he couldn't find one, he was perfectly entitled to claim that the mark was invisible, and, you guessed it, you were found to be a witch …

There were plenty of other similarly inescapable ways of proving that someone was a witch, and thousands of innocent people, mostly women, were killed. Estimates for the number of people executed in Europe for participating in witchcraft vary from 12,000 right up to 100,000; more 'moderate' estimates come in at 60,000.

Elizabeth I passed a Witchcraft Act in 1563, and James I in particular seemed to have a special interest in witches: as James VI of Scotland not only did he appoint royal commissions whose single task was to hunt witches down, but he's known to have participated in witch trials too. In 1597 he published a treatise on witchcraft called *Daemonologie*, although by this time he'd begun an about-turn in his thinking, and revoked those earlier royal commissions.

By the time he had assumed the throne as James I of England, it seems he had become more sceptical of the witch trials, and despite introducing his own, harsher

Witch Craft Act in 1604, it was never used in his reign.

A time, then, when even if you were thought to be *associated* with a witch you could end up trying to hold your breath under water for a very long time, when even greater atrocities were taking place abroad, *and* a Scots king (known for his interest in all things witchy) takes the English throne ...

... and Shakespeare writes a play with witches in the first scene, who then lead a man to commit high treason.

Topical.

We may laugh at witches nowadays; indeed, their scenes in *Macbeth* are often thought to be the hardest to get right in modern productions. They're usually the least scary moments, too: we're simply not afraid of witches any more.

Although we may know that the witch trials of a few hundred years ago were truly horrific, we don't have access to the kind of fear the Elizabethans would have had, the continual suspicion, not only a terror of witches themselves but an entire ideology that poured from that fear into the minds of the populace – it made people paranoid and trigger-happy, crying *Witch!* at anybody with a crooked thumb.

For an Elizabethan audience, playing an ace and opening the play with the scariest characters is a pretty gutsy thing to do. Without working out why the witches are there, it's too easy to dismiss them as worthless plot devices. But Shakespeare uses the witches to help set the tone, and for his audience, they'd be very quickly aware that the tone is a bloody scary one.

Think of a witch now, and some green-skinned, wart-nosed hag from *The Wizard of Oz* (1939) will probably come to mind. A *Dr Who* episode in 2007 set in Shakespeare's London featured witches; they were slightly green-skinned, but they also had pointy teeth and, well, they did scare me. *Dr Who* has always terrified me, though.

But to get an idea of how terrifying witches would have been to an Elizabethan audience, and how strange and unreal they would seem, bear this in mind: 200 years after Shakespeare was alive (100 or so years after the witch-hunts were over), people were only just *beginning* to draw witches. Until that point, it seems, they wouldn't have been comfortable depicting them.

In 2006 at the Tate Britain in London, there was an exhibition called 'Gothic Nightmares'. It wasn't so scary. I wandered through the first half of the exhibition not really appreciating the paintings of imps and ghouls, ghosts and witches sitting on the edge of beds, swirling above someone sleeping, very often visiting someone in prison or surprising someone on a heath.

I found a dark room where a modern projector had been set up to replicate an 18th-century projector – crude cut-out shapes were being placed before a bulb that was being made to flicker like a candle, making cartoon-ish images float from side to side on the wall opposite. It was boring.

Then, out of the middle distance, a pair of yellow eyes loomed.

The eyes belonged to a face that rushed towards me so quickly I tried to jump out of the way.

Fortunately it was dark, so no one saw me make a fool of myself. As I left the room I glanced at my friend who, I was glad to see, also looked a little, ahem, spooked.

I stopped to think. I had been scared by cardboard and light. Me, with my 21st-century head, used to all manner of special effects, horror movies, blood and gore on TV and in the cinema.

If it can scare us, what must it have done to people living 200 years ago, when these images were first made? How terrifying would it be to see a picture move, animatedly? To be sure, if you could take a TV back in time 200 years and show it to someone on the street, their mind probably wouldn't be able to comprehend what it was seeing.

So I made my way back to the beginning of the exhibition and started again, this time trying to imagine what it must have been like for someone from the 18th century to see these pictures for the first time, to have their nightmares, their worst fears, put into pictorial form.

I came across a painting of a man on a heath, meeting three witches. I thought of this book.

I went back to the beginning of the gallery a third time, and started again, this time trying as hard as I could to dismiss my modern head, and replace it with an Elizabethan's.

Take a TV 200 years into the past, and you'd freak people out. Take it 400 years back and they'd put you to the stake. Take an Elizabethan 200 years into the future, into the 18th century, show them these paintings, and they'd freak out.

So I was scared. The people in the 18th century, seeing the worst things imaginable suddenly given shape, would have been scared.

What must the idea of actual, real live witches have been like to the Elizabethans?

400 years ago, Shakespeare took his audience and put witches in front of them, which was a pretty ballsy thing to do. They would have found them very terrifying and very real.

And that's how you have to think when you come into contact with Shakespeare. You have to think the way an Elizabethan would.

Shakespeare said everything. Brain to belly; every mood and minute of a man's season. His language is starlight and fireflies and the sun and the moon. He wrote it with tears and blood and beer, and his words march like heart-beats. He speaks to everyone and we all claim him, but it's wise to remember, if we would really appreciate him, that he doesn't properly belong to us but to another world that smelled assertively of columbine and gun powder and printer's ink and was vigorously dominated by Elizabeth.

Orson Welles, *Everybody's Shakespeare*, 1934

Scene 7

A castle, Scotland, 11th century

I've gone into the witches in depth, even though I'm not going to look at a witches' scene. When we realise how horrifically, bone-shakingly fearsome the Elizabethans would have found the witches, their scenes begin to make sense, and it makes it easier to understand why Macbeth believes what they say: he's told right at the beginning by the witches that he will be king; this starts a domino effect that leads to him killing his king. By listening to their predictions and following their advice, Macbeth is essentially selling his soul to the devil, and that, the Elizabethans knew in the core of their beings, was a surefire path to destruction.

Without any further ado, let's look at the extract. It's Act 2, Scene 2, and it begins with Lady Macbeth waiting nervously for her husband to return from killing the king ...

Enter LADY MACBETH

LADY MACBETH
That which hath made them drunk hath made me bold;
What hath quench'd them hath given me fire.

Hark! Peace!
It was the owl that shriek'd, the fatal bellman,
Which gives the stern'st good-night. He is about it:
The doors are open; and the surfeited grooms
Do mock their charge with snores: I have drugg'd
their possets,
That death and nature do contend about them,
Whether they live or die.

MACBETH
[*Within*] Who's there? what, ho!

LADY MACBETH
Alack, I am afraid they have awaked,
And 'tis not done. The attempt and not the deed
Confounds us. Hark! I laid their daggers ready;
He could not miss 'em. Had he not resembled
My father as he slept, I had done't.

Enter MACBETH

My husband!

MACBETH
I have done the deed. Didst thou not hear a noise?

LADY MACBETH
I heard the owl scream and the crickets cry.
Did not you speak?

MACBETH
When?

LADY MACBETH
Now.

MACBETH
As I descended?

Actually, stop there. I don't want to work from this edition of the text. There are hundreds of different editions of Shakespeare available, both online and in shops. This layout is from an online edition of the play that shall remain nameless, though it saddens me to say it's touted for students and educators.

To be fair, after all my First Folio trumpet-blowing, the Folio text of *Macbeth* has the same layout. The Folio does have its faults, particularly that the space constraints in printing the book meant that the metre couldn't always be laid out as the actors may have wanted.

Now take a look below at the way the text is laid out in the Penguin edition. You'll find this layout (though not the spelling) in any one of the major publishing house editions of the plays. I've kept the spellings from the Folio, because I like them, but also because anything that helps to remember that this is an old story from an old time is a Good Thing:

[*Enter Lady.*]

La.
That which hath made the[m] drunk, hath made me bold:
What hath quench'd them, hath giuen me fire.
Hearke, peace: it was the Owle that shriek'd,
The fatall Bell-man, which giues the stern'st good-night.
He is about it, the Doores are open:
And the surfeted Groomes doe mock their charge
With Snores. I haue drugg'd their Possets,
That Death and Nature doe contend about them,
Whether they liue, or dye.

[*Enter Macbeth.*]

Macb.
                              Who's there? what hoa?

Lady
Alack, I am afraid they haue awak'd,
And 'tis not done: th' attempt, and not the deed,
Confounds vs: hearke: I lay'd their Daggers ready,
He could not misse 'em. Had he not resembled
My Father as he slept, I had don't.
My Husband?

Macb.
I haue done the deed:
Didst thou not heare a noyse?

Lady
I heard the Owle schreame, and the Crickets cry.
Did not you speake?

Macb.
                   When?

Lady
                        Now.

Macb.
                                   As I descended?

Lady
I.

Macb.
Hearke!
Who lyes i'th' second Chamber?

Lady
                                   Donalbaine.

Macb.
This is a sorry sight.

Lady
A foolish thought, to say a sorry sight.

Macb.
There's one did laugh in's sleepe,
And one cry'd Murther, that they did wake each other:
I stood, and heard them: But they did say their Prayers,
And addrest them againe to sleepe.

Lady
There are two lodg'd together.

Macb.
One cry'd God blesse vs, and Amen the other,
As they had seene me with these Hangmans hands:
Listning their feare, I could not say Amen,
When they did say God blesse vs.

Lady
Consider it not so deepely.

Macb.
But wherefore could not I pronounce Amen?
I had most need of Blessing, and Amen
Stuck in my throat.

Lady
                    These deeds must not be thought
After these wayes: so, it will make vs mad.

You can see there are a number of differences between the
two versions I've shown you. I'm not even going to start

talking about the number of extra exclamation marks there are in the online version, because I may begin to rant, and that will do no good.

Obviously the spellings in the second version are a little odd, but once you get used to the letter *u* printed as a *v*, the *j* printed as *i*, and the extra *e* scattered about, it isn't so hard. This second version of the text is the one that Shakespeare's actors would have authorised, had they the printing space.

They would want the text to be laid out as they remembered it, which is to say for the purposes of performing, and we can work out from the metre how that would look. As it's unlikely there were directors in those days, Shakespeare would have had to write into the text his directions for his actors – actors he had worked with for years, whose strengths and weaknesses he knew he could write to.

Scene 8

221b Baker Street

There is, of course, no one interpretation of any piece. You can make your own, if you like. But first, I'm going to take you through mine.

The first clue is to examine the metre.

You'll remember from Act 4 that Shakespeare wrote many of his plays almost entirely in verse, and that when he wrote in verse he wrote mostly in iambic pentameter, and that in iambic pentameter lines of verse have ten syllables in them. Supposedly.

So. Exercise Number One.

Let's go through the scene from *Macbeth* and count how many syllables there are in each line. As this is supposed to be in iambic pentameter, we'd expect every line to have ten syllables.

When a line of metre is shared by two characters, I've marked the second half of the line to show how it makes up ten syllables (and so a complete line of pentameter), e.g. 7–10. I've also marked lines as 9/10 or 10/11, to show that depending on how you articulate a word in that line, the number of syllables can change slightly:

Act 5, Scene 8

[*Enter Lady.*]

Lady

10   That which hath made the[m] drunk, hath made me bold:
9/10 What hath quench'd them, hath giuen me fire.
8   Hearke, peace: it was the Owle that shriek'd,
11   The fatall Bell-man, which giues the stern'st good-night.
10   He is about it, the Doores are open:
10   And the surfeted Groomes doe mock their charge
8   With Snores. I haue drugg'd their Possets,
10/11 That Death and Nature doe contend about them,
6   Whether they liue, or dye.

[*Enter Macbeth.*]

Macb.

7–10   Who's there? what hoa?

Lady

10   Alack, I am afraid they haue awak'd,
10   And 'tis not done: th' attempt, and not the deed,
11   Confounds vs: hearke: I lay'd their Daggers ready,
11   He could not misse 'em. Had he not resembled
9   My Father as he slept, I had don't.
3   My Husband?

Macb.

5   I haue done the deed:
6   Didst thou not heare a noyse?

Lady

10   I heard the Owle schreame, and the Crickets cry.

4   Did not you speake?

Macb.

5   When?

Lady

6   Now.

Macb.

7–11   As I descended?

Lady

1   I.

Macb.

1   Hearke!

7   Who lyes i'th' second Chamber?

Lady

8–10   *Donalbaine.*

Macb.

6   This is a sorry sight.

Lady

10   A foolish thought, to say a sorry sight.

Macb.

6   There's one did laugh in's sleepe,

12   And one cry'd Murther, that they did wake each other:

11   I stood, and heard them: But they did say their Prayers,

8   And addrest them againe to sleepe.

Lady

7   There are two lodg'd together.

Macb.

11   One cry'd God blesse vs, and Amen the other,

10   As they had seene me with these Hangmans hands:

10   Listning their feare, I could not say Amen,

7   When they did say God blesse vs.

Lady

8   Consider it not so deepely.

Macb.

10   But wherefore could not I pronounce Amen?

10   I had most need of Blessing, and Amen

4   Stuck in my throat.

Lady

6–10   These deeds must not be thought

10   After these wayes: so, it will make vs mad.

When a scene is written in metre, and the words don't start

on the far left of the page underneath the character name, like in the lines 'When?/Now./As I descended?', then they are not new lines of metre, but *shared lines*, which we looked at briefly in Act 4 – one line of metre broken up and shared across two or more characters:

> *Macb.*
>
> 7   Who lyes I'th' second Chamber?
>
> *Lady*
>
> 8–10   *Donalbaine.*

Which makes up a perfect ten.

As you can see from my syllable count, there are a lot of lines that don't make up a perfect ten. Plenty of lines, in fact, that are far from having ten syllables.

In fact, as we're getting all numerical, in 34 lines of text, there are only twelve pure, unbroken lines of pentameter. That's a little odd, isn't it …?

If we include shared lines, or lines that could be made ten if we work them a little when speaking them, the total can reach seventeen. But even if we do include those extras, that means there are still seventeen lines that have been messed about with, and that are either a little under ten syllables, or a little over.

Let's not underestimate the significance of these sums.

If something is supposed to have ten syllables in it, then it should have ten syllables in it. Period.

Shakespeare, when he wrote this, was intending to write in iambic pentameter. And he *is*. But like a jazz musician, he plays around the riff of ten syllables.

Take Lady's first speech again:

> *Lady*
>
> 10   That which hath made the[m] drunk, hath made me bold:
> 9/10 What hath quench'd them, hath giuen me fire.
> 8   Hearke, peace: it was the Owle that shriek'd,
> 11   The fatall Bell-man, which giues the stern'st good-night.
> 10   He is about it, the Doores are open:
> 10   And the surfeted Groomes doe mock their charge
> 8   With Snores. I haue drugg'd their Possets,
> 10/11 That Death and Nature doe contend about them,
> 6   Whether they liue, or dye.
>
> [*Enter Macbeth.*]
>
> *Macb.*
> 7–10   Who's there? what hoa?

Look at the syllable counts! Shakespeare starts with a ten – this is the melody, the main tune that he's going to play with – then he plays another ten (though it could be spoken as a nine if you speak the word *fire* monosyllabically), then a cheeky eight, whacks it up to eleven, back to ten for two lines (to remind you of the tune), down to another cheeky eight, up to a ten/eleven (*about'em/about them*), and then to finish the speech, a ten (though it's split by a line break).

Look at it this way:

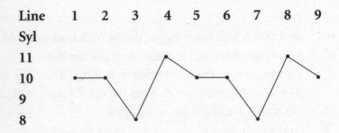

He's riffing. Miles Davis eat your heart out! Remember that he's supposed to be writing in iambic pentameter, so the speech *should* look like this:

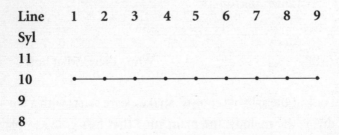

Take a look at the scene as a whole in this way (Figures 1 and 2 opposite):

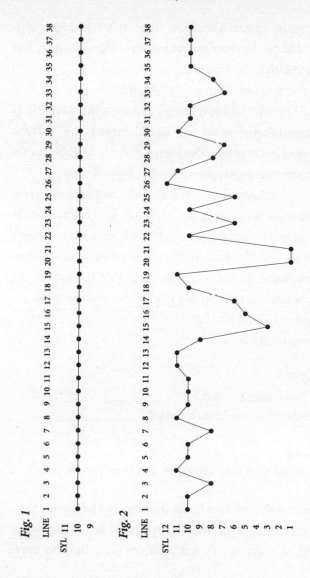

The entire extract should, if absolutely sticking to regular iambic pentameter structure, look like Figure 1. But actually it looks like Figure 2.

Yes, I've too much time on my hands.

Full of murder and suspense, it's an incredibly emotionally charged scene, so, as you would expect, the metre is very irregular. Or rather, the metre is very irregular, so we know it's an incredibly emotionally charged scene.

But what advantage does the irregular metre give Shakespeare, and more to the point, his actors and his audience?

At the end of Act 4, I touched on the idea that if there's a line of six syllables followed by a line of ten syllables then the actor *has* to fill the two-beat space that is left after the six but before the new line of ten, to observe the metre.

Numbers, numbers …

This is what I mean:

Macb.

5   I haue done the deed: _____⌐

6   Didst thou not heare a noyse? _____⌐

Lady

10   I heard the Owle schreame, and the Crickets cry.

The scene is written in what is supposed to be iambic pentameter, and the basic steady rhythm of ten syllables per line. When there aren't ten syllables in a line, to carry straight on, ignoring the underlying rhythm, would wreck the pace of the scene that Shakespeare intended.

The actor playing Macbeth, speaking the lines above, should say 'I have done the deed', then should try to fill the following 2½ beats (five syllables) somehow: he could move to Lady Macbeth, he could look scared, he could listen out to hear if anyone is raising the alarm. Then, when he's done that, after he says 'Didst thou not heare a noyse?' there's another pause of two beats (to complete his line), before Lady can give her line. Perhaps she gets frustrated with him panicking. Or they both stand there listening …

The point is, for the actor playing Macbeth to run his two lines together, and Lady to come in immediately after Macbeth's last line, would be to ignore the clues given by the metre.

I haue done the deed, didst thou not heare a noyse? I heard the Owle schreame …

And if the metre wasn't important, if it wasn't there to fill some function, Shakespeare would have written it in prose.

There are at least two good things that come from Shakespeare breaking the metre up like this. The break gives the actors time to act, react, move across the stage, do a bit of stage business, show the audience how their character is feeling, whatever. They're pauses for 'reaction shots', I suppose you would say, to steal a term from the movie business, and these breaks are good clues to the actors that something more is going on, beneath the plain speaking of the words.

But they also set the pace of the scene. Whether you give the character one beat or 4½ beats will determine how soon it will be before they say their next line, or how quickly the character they're speaking to will start speaking *their* lines …

Take a look at the scene from *Macbeth* again – I've filled in the gaps in the metre, to clearly mark out where a bit of stage business (or a pause, or silence) is needed to keep the metrical rhythm steadily bouncing along:

    Lady

10	That which hath made the[m] drunk, hath made me bold:
9/10	What hath quench'd them, hath giuen me fire.
8	Hearke, peace: it was the Owle that shriek'd, _____
11	The fatall Bell-man, which giues the stern'st good-night.
10	He is about it, the Doores are open:
10	And the surfeted Groomes doe mock their charge
8	With Snores. I haue drugg'd their Possets, _____
10/11	That Death and Nature doe contend about them,
6	Whether they liue, or dye.

    [*Enter Macbeth.*]

    Macb.

7–10	Who's there? what hoa?

Lady

10 Alack, I am afraid they haue awak'd,

10 And 'tis not done: th' attempt, and not the deed,

11 Confounds vs: hearke: I lay'd their Daggers ready,

11 He could not misse 'em. Had he not resembled

9 My Father as he slept, I had don't. _____|

3 My Husband? _____|

Macb.

5 I haue done the deed: _____|

6 Didst thou not heare a noyse? _____|

Lady

10 I heard the Owle schreame, and the Crickets cry.

4 Did not you speake?

Macb.

5   When?

Lady

6   Now.

Macb.

7–11   As I descended?

Lady

1 I. _____|

Macb.

1   Hearke! _____|

7   Who lyes i'th' second Chamber?

Lady

8–10   Donalbaine.

Macb.

6   This is a sorry sight. _____|

Lady

10   A foolish thought, to say a sorry sight.

Macb.

6   There's one did laugh in's sleepe, _____|

12   And one cry'd Murther, that they did wake each other:

11   I stood, and heard them: But they did say their Prayers,

8   And addrest them againe to sleepe. _____|

Lady

7   There are two lodg'd together. _____|

Macb.

11   One cry'd God blesse vs, and Amen the other,

10   As they had seene me with these Hangmans hands:

10   Listning their feare, I could not say Amen,

7   When they did say God blesse vs. _____|

Lady

8   Consider it not so deepely. _____|

Macb.

10   But wherefore could not I pronounce Amen?
10   I had most need of Blessing, and Amen
4   Stuck in my throat.

Lady

6–10   These deeds must not be thought
10   After these wayes: so, it will make vs mad.

I've said it before, and I'll say it again, Miles Davis, eat your heart out ...

Now what do you do with all those gaps and pauses?

The little 'O'

Talking of moments to show character, something you'll find a lot of in Shakespeare's plays is the letter *O*:

O that this too too sullied flesh would melt
O all you host of Heaven! O Earth; what else?
O what a Rogue and Peasant slave am I?

... to take three examples from a chap who says it rather a lot (Hamlet). With this little letter, Shakespeare practically gives an actor *carte blanche* to do, well, whatever they like. It is, for want of a better way to explain it, a blank space, a sign to tell the actor to vocally signal their emotional response. Sigh. Express contempt. Or frustration. Or relief. Make it brief or drag it out, but whatever you do, use it and don't just say 'Oh'. All together now, *Ohhhhh for a Muse of Fire ...*

Scene 9

The London Underground

Well, there are plenty of things you could do with all those gaps and pauses, which is one of the reasons why Shakespeare is performed so much and his plays are open to endless interpretation. What is written below is my interpretation, and by no means do I list all the possible thoughts and feelings that may or may not be running through these two characters' heads. It's not a definitive analysis, it's one of many.

If you're a playwright and you're writing in iambic pentameter, and you want your character to sound calm and sane and clear, you might write their speeches using clear and simple words, with thoughts that finish at the end of a line of metre.

Conversely, if you want to express a character's angst, their stress, their worries and their confusion, yes, you could just have them say, 'Ooh I'm feeling a little stressed and confused right now', or you could have them talk about something completely different, but make them say it in a very complicated way. This is what Shakespeare does with Lady Macbeth's first speech in this scene.

Let's look at it:

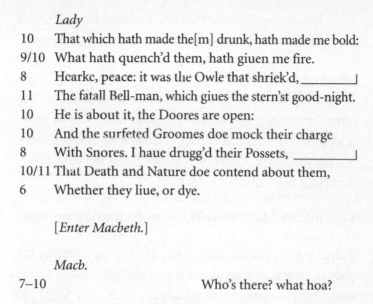

Lady

10   That which hath made the[m] drunk, hath made me bold:

9/10 What hath quench'd them, hath giuen me fire.

8   Hearke, peace: it was the Owle that shriek'd, _____⌡

11   The fatall Bell-man, which giues the stern'st good-night.

10   He is about it, the Doores are open:

10   And the surfeted Groomes doe mock their charge

8   With Snores. I haue drugg'd their Possets, _____⌡

10/11 That Death and Nature doe contend about them,

6   Whether they liue, or dye.

[*Enter Macbeth.*]

Macb.

7–10   Who's there? what hoa?

The first two sentences are simple, and essentially say the same thing: what made them (the King's guards) drunk, made me strong. What has exhausted them, has given me fire.

But wait a second – what kind of person repeats the same thing over and over? 'To bed, to bed, to bed …' as she says later in the play (once she's gone mad). She's telling us that she's not nervous, that she's been calmed by a quick swig of alcohol. And the metre, in two lines of ten, would support that. But she's repeating herself, so maybe she is a *little* nervous. Then:

8   Hearke, peace: it was the Owle that shriek'd, _____|
11   The fatall Bell-man, which giues the stern'st good-night.

Hearke means *listen. Peace* in this instance means *forget about it, it was nothing.* She hears a noise that makes her jump, completely belying her previous statement of boldness, not two lines before. She's so nervous that a shrieking owl made her think it was the sound of the king dying. A curious line follows:

11   The fatall Bell-man, which giues the stern'st good-night.

Which is a pretty odd thing to say. After being scared by the owl, she starts talking about it in a melodramatic, poetic way. This is something that Lady seems to do a lot of (in her first meeting with Duncan in Act 1, Scene 6, she gets so nervous she ends her speech with the somewhat peculiar 'We rest your hermits'). She's reassuring herself, perhaps making a joke about the fact that it scared her, calling it a *fatal bellman.* An owl *was* said to be a harbinger of doom; hearing its call was considered bad luck. So if she is joking, it's a very black humour. The 'joke' calms her, and in the next two lines of ten she thinks about her husband – has he killed Duncan yet? Is he about to? What about the guards? Will they catch him?

She tells us the guards are sleeping, and with the midline ending, excitedly interrupts herself to tell us she put something in their drinks to make them sleep:

10   He is about it, the Doores are open:
10   And the surfeted Groomes doe mock their charge
8   With Snores. I haue drugg'd their Possets, _____|

Perhaps she's nervous, or proud of the part she played –
whatever the reason, she remembers the drugs, then imagines Death and Nature fighting over the sleeping guards:

8   With Snores. I haue drugg'd their Possets, _____|
10/11 That Death and Nature doe contend about them,
6   Whether they liue, or dye.

Immediately, her husband calls as he enters – he's heard
someone talking: this is one of Shakespeare's clues. His two
characters (unknowingly, in this instance) share a complete line of metre:

6   Whether they liue, or dye.

      [*Enter Macbeth.*]

      Macb.
7–10   Who's there? what hoa?

He wants the actors to pick up their cues here – to not let

there be a gap between one character speaking and the other. No pause, in other words, between Lady Macbeth saying *live, or dye*, and Macbeth entering and calling out.

This is indisputable: the scene is written in metre. The rhythm is bouncing along and the audience is tuned into it. If Macbeth doesn't speak right on cue, it will upset the rhythm of the metre. If he does, the metrical rhythm can continue unbroken.

If Shakespeare had wanted a pause between the lines, he'd have put one in, as we'll see in a moment. There's a clearer example coming up, but this is the beginning of Shakespeare orchestrating the dramatic intensity of the scene, through the metre.

A moment ago I said that the two characters unknowingly share a line of metre. It seems clear from what's said that when Macbeth calls 'Who's there? what hoa?', Lady doesn't see him, or perhaps doesn't hear him properly, because she has a further six lines before they start talking to each other; plus the speech ends with her calling out and asking if it's Macbeth approaching.

This is the first real unspoken stage direction from Shakespeare. He wants Macbeth onstage, perhaps in shock, but visible to the audience; and more to the point, out of sight of Mrs Macbeth.

Whatever it is that she thinks she heard when he called has scared her, and the one thing she didn't talk about

directly in her previous speech (but seems to have been on
her mind) she finally vocalises:

> *Lady*
> 10   Alack, I am afraid they haue awak'd,
> 10   And 'tis not done: th' attempt, and not the deed,
> 11   Confounds vs: hearke: I lay'd their Daggers ready,
> 11   He could not misse 'em. Had he not resembled
> 9   My Father as he slept, I had don't. _____|
> 3   My Husband? _____|

She's still talking to the audience, and begins by saying *Oh
no, the guards have woken, he hasn't killed Duncan, he's been
caught and we're going to get busted for trying to kill him,
rather than actually killing him.* She carries on fretting to
herself/the audience:

>   th' attempt, and not the deed,
> 11   Confounds vs: hearke: I lay'd their Daggers ready,
> 11   He could not misse 'em.

Worried that they have been caught in the act, she calls
hearke again, interrupting her own fretting, thinking she
heard a noise (she probably did hear something this time
– perhaps her husband returning). Immediately, either
reassuring us or herself, she tells us she placed the daggers
carefully for Macbeth to find, implying everything should
be going well …

A curious way to commit a murder, leaving the intended murder weapons for anybody to find. If she put the daggers in place, why didn't she do it herself? As we heard in Act 1 of *Macbeth*, it's at her insistence that they're doing this at all. We hear her reason straight away:

> Had he not resembled
> 9   My Father as he slept, I had don't. _____⌟

I've always thought it interesting that when she refers to her father, it's a nine-syllable line – and because of the contraction, *intentionally* a nine-syllable line. Without the contraction (*done it* instead of *don't*) it would be an even ten.

What deep psychological trauma lies in that simple sentence? When she saw Duncan sleeping, as she laid the daggers next to him for Macbeth to find, she says he looked like her father ... Does this remind her of her own father's death for some reason? Is that what drives her mad, eventually, a twisted idea that she's killed her own father?

Whatever the reason, it's a cheeky little slice of backstory for an actor, and writing it in a nine-syllable line means there's a half-beat before the next line where the actor can pause, reflect, think of *something*, and in so doing give the audience a momentary glimpse into the character's life.

Then she breaks from her thoughts, hears him, calls to him. But he doesn't immediately reply:

3   My Husband? _____|

     Macb.
5   I haue done the deed: _____|
6   Didst thou not heare a noyse? _____|

This is a fascinating little piece of writing. Either she still can't see him yet, doesn't recognise him, or perhaps is worried that the person coming towards her *isn't* Macbeth. Not only that, he doesn't reassure her straight away: *My Husband?* she asks – a three-syllable line, meaning he waits 3½ beats before he responds. Why does he wait? That's a question for the actor. Perhaps he's nervous. Perhaps he's listening for the guards, or crossing the stage to whisper to her. Perhaps he's completely freaking out. Whatever the reason, finally he says:

     Macb.
5   I haue done the deed: _____|

And then pauses for another 2½ beats. He listens again. Then asks her:

     Macb.
6   Didst thou not heare a noyse? _____|

She doesn't reply immediately. She waits two beats before answering. Think about that. Two people, standing in near-dark, in a castle. One has just killed the king. Both are nervous as all hell, and straining to hear if they've been caught.

     Macb.
6   Didst thou not heare a noyse? _____ ⌐

She waits. Thinks or listens. Then she says:

     Lady
10   I heard the Owle schreame, and the Crickets cry.
4   Did not you speake?

A beautiful line of ten. *Owle **scream**, **crickets** **cry**.* Great bit of poetry. The words she uses sound like the owl and cricket noises she thought she heard during her speech earlier, *cr-cr-cr* …

Then she asks, *Did you just say something?* And Shakespeare, deciding they're not tense enough, gets them *really* worked up:

     Lady
4   Did not you speake?

     Macb.
5   When?

	Lady	
6		Now.

	Macb.	
7–11		As I descended?

	Lady	
1	I._____

This is really wonderful writing. Look at the staggered, shared speech that looks like a stairway, ending with the words *As I descended?* Shakespeare shares one line of iambic pentameter between two characters, over four speeches. The actors *must*, in order to keep the metrical rhythm, immediately respond to each other, jumping on each others' words.

Speak those four speeches out loud as one unbroken line, no pausing or punctuation:

Did not you speake when now as I descended

That's how fast it should be said. It's machine-gun fast, and Shakespeare, knowing that his actors knew how metre worked, tells them to say it that fast, without any need of actually writing stage directions down. He's speaking to them through the metre.

It's the closest thing to Shakespeare's voice we have, closer than any of the sonnets where he writes so much in the first person. When you find these directions in Shakespeare's plays, it's almost like a bearded voice whispers over your shoulder, 'Do it like *that* …'

But we need to step back a line or two. We've missed something small, but noteworthy. Macbeth asks Lady

> *Macb.*
> Didst **thou** not heare a noyse? _____

And she replies:

> *Lady*
> I heard the Owle schreame, and the Crickets cry.
> Did not **you** speake?

He uses the *thou* of special intimacy, the pet name, to her. She uses the more formal *you* to him, as she has done ever since he tried to talk her out of the murder, and as she does until she dies …

Immediately after that rat-a-tat-tat shared line, Lady Macbeth begins a new line of metre with one word, 'I' …

And they both stop still …

> *Lady*
> 4   Did not you speake?

Macb.
5   When?

Lady
6   Now.

Macb.
7–11   As I descended?

Lady
1   I._____|

… they're both fiercely listening for any sound that might let them know they've been caught killing God, or that someone might have heard them speaking to each other. Nine syllables – 4½ beats – that's a lot of stage time, especially after the quick-fire exchange. After the rapidity of the shared line, a great pause. Then Macbeth comes in with his line and we have *another* 4½ beat silence:

Lady
1   I._____|

Macb.
1   Hearke!_____|
7   Who lyes i'th' second Chamber?

If the previous lines are performed to follow the metre,

and the intensity is there, then Lady Macbeth's 'I' followed by the silence as they listen, followed by Macbeth's call of 'Hearke!' (*shut up and listen*) might get a laugh from the audience. It *is* kinda silly. Them both standing there quietly, carefully listening, and then he says *Shush!* Master dramatist that he is, Shakespeare often places moments of comedy in moments of great tragedy, and vice versa. Make your audience laugh, and you'll make them cry even harder.

So they listen for another 4½. Then something makes him think: Who's sleeping next door to Duncan? Could that be what we think we can hear? Did someone sleeping next door hear the murder and wake up? Lady Macbeth finishes the line of metre, answering immediately:

Macb.

1   Hearke! _____|

7   Who lyes i'th' second Chamber?

Lady

8–10   *Donalbaine.*

Why does she answer immediately? Why isn't there a pause after *Chamber*? The metre demands that Lady comes in on cue, and, bearing in mind that this is her house (well, castle), and they've planned to murder the king, of course she's going to know who's sleeping where.

Macb.

6   This is a sorry sight._____|

Lady

10   A foolish thought, to say a sorry sight.

He replies to her answer of 'Donalbaine' with a very sad line, 'This is a sorry sight'. We know he isn't showing her that he's brought the daggers back with him, because she doesn't seem to see them until the rather straightforward line of ten a bit later on: 'Why did you bring these daggers from the place?'

Perhaps they're still far away from each other onstage. It's very likely to be quite dark – why would the torches still be lit so late at night when everyone should be in bed? Perhaps he's staring at his bloody hands, thinking of Donalbaine (Duncan's son) now sleeping next door to his dead father. Perhaps he's talking about the two of them, terrified of being caught, condemned to an eternity in hell even if they do survive long enough to rule as king and queen for a few years. Whatever action is taking place, after he says 'This is a sorry sight', there's a pause of two beats before she responds with another line of ten syllables.

Lady

10   A foolish thought, to say a sorry sight.

That's a stupid thing to say, she says, after a moment's pause. Perhaps she's getting control of her nerves more quickly than he is. If he were to reply in likewise fashion, in a line of ten, we might think he was calming down too. But he doesn't.

Macb.
6   There's one did laugh in's sleepe, _____⌋
12   And one cry'd Murther, that they did wake each other:
11   I stood, and heard them: But they did say their Prayers,
8   And addrest them againe to sleepe. _____⌋

He goes from one extreme to another, a line of six syllables (and so a pause of four) then a line of twelve. Then an eleven, followed by an eight. He's metrically all over the place, so the actor should take that as the cue for Macbeth's mental state too; he's having trouble recounting the story to her.

There's a short pause, again, before Lady Macbeth says something rather odd:

Lady
7   There are two lodg'd together. _____⌋

If you think about it, that really is quite an odd thing to say. Macbeth has been talking about the guards, so although Lady's comment (if she's referring to the guards) isn't entirely out of context, it's the kind of thing you'd expect your grandmother to say after one too many glasses of port.

Perhaps she means the 'two lodg'd together' (*two sleeping in the same room*) are the noise she heard earlier. Perhaps it's simply an affirmation of what her husband said. But she waits a beat to say it, and then there's another pause before he speaks. For some reason, her comment seems listless.

Then there's yet another pause before Macbeth says something else – he talks about the guards. So it seems they *are* both talking about the guards, but there's something not quite right about what they're saying.

Then it hits you. They're not really listening to each other:

> *Macb.*
>
> 11 I stood, and heard them: But they did say their Prayers,
> 8   And addrest them againe to sleepe. _____|

> *Lady*
>
> 7   There are two lodg'd together. _____|

> *Macb.*
>
> 11 One cry'd God blesse vs, and Amen the other,
> 10 As they had seene me with these Hangmans hands:

They're both talking, and you assume (as there isn't anyone else there to talk to, other than the audience) that they're talking to each other. But, rather sadly, they seem trapped in their own thoughts and fears.

The next part is heartbreaking. Macbeth, when he approached Duncan's room, heard the guards' call *God bless us*, and the normal response *Amen*, but wasn't able to join in. Which is probably just as well, as he wouldn't have wanted to wake them. Waking them doesn't seem as important to him as the blessing, though, and you can almost hear his desperation in the alliterative ***Hangmans hands***:

Macb.

11	One cry'd God blesse vs, and Amen the other,
10	As they had seene me with these Hangmans hands:
10	Listning their feare, I could not say Amen,
7	When they did say God blesse vs. _____⌋

Lady

8	Consider it not so deepely. _____⌋

After a line of seven, he stops, cannot continue speaking. Lady sees him struggle, and says *Don't think so much about it*. Then there's a pause before, out of the depths of himself, Macbeth asks her again.

Macb.

10	But wherefore could not I pronounce Amen?
10	I had most need of Blessing, and Amen
4	Stuck in my throat.

    Lady
6–10   These deeds must not be thought
10   After these wayes: so, it will make vs mad.

He asks her in two careful lines of ten, but it has taken him that pause beforehand to summon up the energy to spit it out. (Note that the important word *Blessing* has a capital *B* in the Folio spelling.)

He doesn't finish, perhaps can't finish his third line of metre, and Lady jumps in, finishing the line of ten and adding another. Her two lines of ten could be seen as her taking control, but how right she is. *Don't think about what you've done in this way, or it will drive us mad …*

And, as you may know, so it does …

This is what separated Shakespeare off from his contemporaries. They all knew about stichomythia, *the Greek term for rapid fire dialogue, but nobody took it down to the level of words and breaths, with his accuracy and ostentation. He wrote speech, not speeches.*

              Dominic Dromgoole, Artistic Director of
Shakespeare's Globe, from his book *Will and Me*, 2006

Winning dialogue

The director and writer Michael Winner said in February 2008 that Shakespeare writes some 'awful' dialogue, and that he defies any actor to speak a certain line of Macduff's in *Macbeth* (Act 4, Scene 3, lines 216–18) and make it believable. Told that Macbeth has had his wife and children slaughtered, Macduff asks over and over again if his wife, his children have all been killed:

> All my pretty ones? Did you say all?
> O hell-kite! All? What, all my pretty chickens
> And their dam, at one fell swoop?

Winner argued that the 'all my pretty chickens' line is impossible to act without causing laughter, and indeed it isn't the easiest of lines to get right. But it isn't awful dialogue. It's *heartbreaking*. The repetition of *all*, the broken lines of metre: spoken with truth, with the right emotion and passion, these lines aren't troublesome, they're a gift. Macduff's whole life has been swept away from him, and Shakespeare brings this tough warrior to his knees, to face a terrible, terrible loss.

Scene 10

Checklist

What I've done with one scene of *Macbeth* you can do with any other scene or play. Not all the scenes of Shakespeare might have so much in them – some may have a lot more – but the methods I've used and the things I've looked for are the keys to unlocking anything that may stand in your way.

Here's a checklist of things to look for:

§ Is the scene in verse or prose? Or both? If both, why does it switch from one to the other?

§ If it's verse, is it regular iambic pentameter, or does the metre jump around all over the place? If it's irregular, what might that be saying about a character's state of mind?

§ Are the speeches complicated or simple – i.e., are there mid-line endings, shared or short lines of metre?
  • If there are mid-line endings, what kind of emotions might be making the characters interrupt themselves?
  • If there are shared lines of metre, what does that say about the characters' relationship?

- If there are short lines of metre, what might the character be doing or thinking in the gap?

§ Do the characters use *thou/you* to each other? If they do, do they switch between the two? If they switch, why do they switch?

§ Are there any characters in the scene that don't speak? Why are they there? How does it help the story to have them there?

That last point is worth picking up on. There are scenes in Shakespeare's plays where characters are mentioned as entering, in the stage directions, yet they say nothing – the infamous spear-carriers. For example, in Act 1, Scene 4 of *King Lear*, the stage direction says *Enter Lear and Attendants* (the Penguin edition says *Enter Lear and Knights*). The Knights don't have much to say, and most, if not all, get sent off to run errands and fetch people. But their presence is a demonstration of Lear's ruling power, as king.

By Act 3, Scene 1, Kent meets a Gentleman on the moor. Lear is howling at the storm, and the Gentleman asks who follows the king. Kent's reply is 'None but the Fool'. A king without followers is no longer king, merely a madman shouting at the wind.

Thank goodness for the spear-carriers.

Epilogue

This book is by no means a complete guide. If it tried to be complete, it would be many times the size, and defeat the whole point. These are some of the basic things you should look for, to crack your way into Shakespeare. The clues will help you break up what may seem like an incomprehensible speech or scene, and give it a clear, dramatic direction. As Cicely Berry, the granddam of voice and Shakespeare once said, there are no rules about how to do Shakespeare, just clues.

There are some who think that 'to follow the metre' too closely can make Shakespeare too cerebral a process, that in so doing you miss the beauty of the words, the dramatic intentions. Others think that everything comes from the metre, that it's the foundation on which to build a character, to let the poetry sing. There are directors who bury their heads in the text, others who barely look at it; actors who base their entire interpretation of a character on the metre, others who see it as a hindrance to their work.

Despite the fact that he was as human, flawed and fallible as the rest of us, the one rule that has always guided me straight and true with Shakespeare is this:

There is always a reason for it.

No matter how complicated, no matter how ostensibly random, how annoying, boring or just plain bad a scene or a line seems to be, there is *always* a reason for it being there.

You just have to find out what it is.

And I promise: the search is always worth it.

Props

Herein ye shall find a chronology of Shakespeare's works, and a list of poetical terms. Be warned, though: the list of poetical terms features some concepts that I didn't discuss in the book, and some are a little tricky.

A chronology of Shakespeare's works

1590–1	*The Two Gentlemen of Verona; The Taming of the Shrew*
1591	*Henry VI Part 2; Henry VI Part 3*
1592	*Henry VI Part 1* (perhaps with Thomas Nashe); *Titus Andronicus* (perhaps with George Peele)
1592–3	*Richard III; Venus and Adonis*
1593–4	*The Rape of Lucrece*
1594	*The Comedy of Errors*
1594–5	*Love's Labour's Lost*
by 1595	*King Edward III*
1595	*Richard II; Romeo and Juliet; A Midsummer Night's Dream*
1596	*King John*
1596–7	*The Merchant of Venice; Henry IV Part 1*
1597–8	*The Merry Wives of Windsor; Henry IV Part 2*

1598	*Much Ado About Nothing*
1598–9	*Henry V*
1599	*Julius Caesar*
1599–1600	*As You Like It*
1600–1	*Hamlet; Twelfth Night*
by 1601	*The Phoenix and the Turtle*
1602	*Troilus and Cressida*
1593–1603	The Sonnets
1603–4	*A Lover's Complaint; Sir Thomas More; Othello*
1603	*Measure for Measure*
1604–5	*All's Well That Ends Well*
1605	*Timon of Athens* (with Thomas Middleton)
1605–6	*King Lear*
1606	*Macbeth* (revised by Middleton); *Antony and Cleopatra*
1607	*Pericles* (with George Wilkins)
1608	*Coriolanus*
1609	*The Winter's Tale*
1610	*Cymbeline*
1611	*The Tempest*
1613	*Henry VIII* (with John Fletcher); *Cardenio* (with John Fletcher)
1613–14	*The Two Noble Kinsmen*

A list of useful concepts for describing Shakespeare's verse (from *The Shakespeare Miscellany*)

English rhythm
In the English language, the basis of rhythm is an alternating contrast between syllables which are perceived to be strong and syllables which are perceived to be weak.

Metre or Meter
The rhythmical organisation of lines of poetry, defined with reference to the number of rhythmical units allowed in a line and by the combinations of strong and weak syllables allowed within those units.

Verse
Any text written in lines which have a metrical structure. The term contrasts with **prose**, where the lines have no predictable rhythmical length or structure, simply reflecting the rhythm of everyday speech.

Prose
Writing that reflects the rhythm of everyday English speech – it doesn't have the issue of rhythmical units and there aren't structured rules for the number of syllables per line.

Blank verse

Verse which has a metrical structure but does not rhyme.

Foot

A unit of rhythm within a metrical line. Lines can consist of any number of feet, but rarely more than six:

monometer	a line consisting of a single foot
dimeter	a line consisting of two feet
trimeter	a line consisting of three feet
tetrameter	a line consisting of four feet
pentameter	a line consisting of five feet
hexameter	a line consisting of six feet

In Shakespeare's works, most lines are pentameters.

Types of foot

There are only so many ways in which strong and weak syllables can be combined to make a foot. Five types are most widely recognised in English verse, but it is not always easy to identify these units in a Shakespearian line, because of the many rhythmical variations found there.

§ *Weak + Strong* – the **iamb** (an **iambic** foot) – the commonest type in English, and the usual one in Shakespeare:
*Once **more**/unto/the **breach**,/dear **friends**,/once **more**,/*

§ *Strong + Weak –* the **trochee** (a **trochaic** foot):
Wherefore / **art** thou / **Rom**eo?

§ *Two Weak + one Strong –* the **anapaest** (an **anapaestic**
foot), spelled **anapest** in American English:
*I am **dead**, / Horatio …*

§ *One Strong + two Weak –* the **dactyl** (a **dactylic** foot):
***See** what a / grace was seated on this brow …*

§ *Two strong –* the **spondee** (a **spondaic** foot):
***On, on,** / you noblest English …*

Feminine ending
Extra unaccented syllables at the end of an iambic or ana-
paestic line of poetry, often used in blank verse:
My lord, as I was sewing in my closet,

Caesura
A rhythmical break in a line of verse, often in the middle
of a line:
To be, or not to be – that is the question
Love? His affections do not that way tend

End-stopped line
A line of verse in which there is a natural pause, suggested

by the meaning, at the end of a line, usually indicated by punctuation:

He took me by the wrist and held me hard.

Run-on lines

A line of verse in which it would be unnatural to pause at the end of a line because the thought continues into the next line:

Whether 'tis nobler in the mind to suffer
The slings and arrows of outrageous fortune …

Stanza

A division of a poem consisting of a series of lines separated from the rest of the poem by lines of white space above and below. In the Shakespearian narrative poems, the stanzas all have the same number of lines and a recurrent pattern of metre and rhyme. In *Venus and Adonis*, for example, each stanza consists of six lines, each in iambic pentameter, with rhymes linking lines 1 / 3, 2 / 4, and 5 / 6. Repeated letters are commonly used to show the rhyming pattern – in this case, *ababcc*. In everyday usage, the term *verse* is loosely used instead of stanza, but this conflicts with the more general meaning of *verse* given above.

Stanza lengths

Stanzas typically run from two to eight lines:

couplet	2 lines
tercet	3 lines
quatrain	4 lines
quintet	5 lines
sestet	6 lines
septet	7 lines
octave	8 lines

Sonnet

A verse form consisting of fourteen lines of iambic penta-meter. In the sonnet form that developed in England, the lines are grouped in three quatrains with six alternating rhymes, followed by a final rhymed couplet:

abab cdcd efef gg.

Supporting Artists
(Recommended Reading)

Playing Shakespeare, by John Barton (Methuen, 1984)

The RSC Shakespeare: The Complete Works, edited by Jonathan Bate and Eric Rasmussen (Palgrave Macmillan, 2007)

Soul of the Age: The Life, Mind and World of William Shakespeare, by Jonathan Bate (Viking 2008)

Think On My Words, by David Crystal (Cambridge University Press, 2008)

Shakespeare's Words, by David Crystal and Ben Crystal (Penguin, 2002)

The Shakespeare Miscellany, by David Crystal and Ben Crystal (Penguin, 2005)

Will and Me, by Dominic Dromgoole (Penguin, 2006)

Shakespeare's Advice to the Players, by Peter Hall (Oberon, 2003)

Speaking Shakespeare, by Patsy Rodenburg (Methuen Drama, 2002)

Secrets of Acting Shakespeare, by Patrick Tucker (Routledge, 2002)

Websites

Online glossary, language companion, and concordance:
  www.shakespeareswords.com

Online edition of the First Folio:
  http://etext.virginia.edu/shakespeare/folio/

Stage Management
(Acknowledgements)

Dedicated, to:

Mum and Dad, for constantly giving their all

My sister Lucy, for always having time to proof-read

Jim Alexander, for keeping me sane in times of metrical madness, and whose notes and suggestions were utterly invaluable

Will Sutton, for talking all this out with me in several bars and cafes around the world

And for Charlotte, who showed me there was more than one way to climb a mountain, and write a book

My deepest thanks to:

My agent Julia Churchill, who hit the bullseye every time

My editor Duncan Heath, for his wise pointers; Andrew Furlow, Najma Finlay, and all at Icon Books, for their tireless work in bringing this book into existence

Adam Russ, for his work on the TV series

Patrick Tucker, for teaching me what it's all *really* about

Patrick Spottiswoode, the Head of Education at Shakespeare's Globe, and his team, the *experts* in bringing down the walls around Shakespeare

Judi Dench, Kenneth Branagh, Richard Eyre, Dominic Dromgoole, Greg Doran, Thelma Holt, Michael Maloney, Sam West, Giles Block, Glynn MacDonald, Annabel Arden, Stanley Wells, Paul Edmondson, Gerald Hewitson, Stan Pretty and Jonathan Milton, and Myrrha Stanford-Smith who have all played such an influential part in getting me to this point

And mes amis: they know who they are, and they know why

Index

Index